Dealing with Resistance in Psychotherapy

Dealing with Resistance in Psychotherapy

Althea J. Horner

JASON ARONSON
Lanham • Boulder • New York • Toronto • Oxford

Published in the United States of America
by Jason Aronson
An imprint of Rowman & Littlefield Publishers, Inc.
A wholly owned subsidiary of
The Rowman & Littlefield Publishing Group, Inc.
4501 Forbes Boulevard, Suite 200, Lanham, Maryland 20706
www.rowmanlittlefield.com

PO Box 317, Oxford OX2 9RU, UK

British Library Cataloguing in Publication Information Available

Library of Congress Cataloging-in-Publication Data Available

ISBN 0-7657-0077-8 (cloth. : alk. paper)

Printed in the United States of America

∞™ The paper used in this publication meets the minimum requirements of
American National Standard for Information Sciences—Permanence of Paper for
Printed Library Materials, ANSI/NISO Z39.48-1992.

Contents

Introduction

A WAY OF THINKING

What I hope to communicate in this book is a *way of thinking* and not a directory of what to do and when to do it. Ultimately, how one applies what is learned here or elsewhere depends on one's own ability to relate, as well as one's level of interpersonal skills and theoretical knowledge. This is a way of thinking that can accommodate more than one theory. *There is, nonetheless, a basic assumption of how we become who we are, which emphasizes the developmental perspective and the relational, interpersonal matrix within which that development takes place*—an assumption rooted in object relations theory. All theories start with the same observations of human behavior, although in each of them the data are organized according to different principles. We may think in terms of psychosexual stages, in terms of Bowlby and a failure or pathology of attachment, in terms of Mahlerian stages of separation and individuation, or in terms of Eriksonian stages of the individual in relation to society. We may think in terms of a Freudian Oedipal conflict, a Kohutian reaction to failure of empathy, a Winnicottian false-self adaptation to impingement, or even in terms of Skinnerian shaping.

There is also the recent work of Allan Schore (1996) and the psychoneurology of development in infancy, the neurological underpinnings of interpersonal attachment, and the capacity to regulate affect and self-soothe. There is the older work of Piaget (1952) as it relates to cognitive functioning in healthy and pathological states and the studies of Chess and Thomas (1971) of constitutionally based differences in the infant.

There is also family systems theory; the philosophy of Buber and the importance of the I–thou encounter with existential questions concerning being itself; language and thought and the search for the individual's meanings embedded in ordinary words, the emphasis on linguistics—all of these are concepts that will enhance our psychoanalytic theory if we allow them into our creative synthesis.

Winnicott (1965) points out that the mother serves as a bridge between the child's experiences of self that originate within him and those that are responses to the external world of reality. If *we view the self as developing within the context of the mother–child matrix*—and this includes all facets of that self, including the way it controls its impulses, uses its potential intellect, or structures reality—*then we can expect to find a correspondence between disturbances of that psychological self and the nature of the relationship with the primary mothering object.* This will be manifest in the developmental history of the individual, in the nature of the individual's inner psychological world, in the quality of present-day relationships and functioning, and, in particular, in the quality of the individual's relationship with the therapist.

Using the concepts of object relations theory, consideration of the basic processes of organization will clarify how the inner mental configurations of the self, the object, and their interrelationships come into being. What is the nature of the process? What is to be organized? What facilitates it? What interferes with it? What is the outcome of its failure? We have to look closely at the baby's own contribution to the process with respect to the kind of brain he or she is born with and how it does its work, what is referred to by ego psychologists as the synthetic function of the ego (Horner [1979] 1984).

There are some cases in which the dominance of the right brain that is manifest in mathematical or musical genius may very well interfere with the child's negotiation of his or her interpersonal milieu and the linguistic frame that dominates it. Many such individuals were notably late talkers (Sowell 1998). It was found that 90 percent of these children are males, that they come from families with a particular cognitive style, and that a majority of the parents are engineers, accountants, computer specialists, and scientists. Many of the children are precocious in music, math, and memory. Some such children have been erroneously diagnosed and treated as retarded or autistic with destructive outcomes for the child and the family. Atypical development will be the result, leading to problems that cannot be laid at the doorstep of an unempathic mother. Obviously such children can be negatively impacted by parents who have their own need to have the child perform well in school from the start or to have the child fit into some desired norm. These parents may also become overly invested in the child's precociousness and neglect the emotional side of the child's development. If in therapy later in life, this individual's very brilliance may come to stand as a resistance. If the therapist, like the parents, is so taken by the patient's intelligence, the therapist will neglect the emotional–relational issues that are buried or repressed—that is, the core relationship problem and the defenses against its exploration.

A pathological grandiose self (Kohut 1971) may become consolidated around the extraordinary talents or intelligence of the individual. It will then stand as the major defense against the terrors of loss of self-cohesion, a persecutory object, or an underlying anaclitic depression. Any attempt to make such an interpretation is most likely to be experienced as an attack on the self, evoking a paranoid reaction. Kohut's approach is most useful with such a patient.

One individual with this character structure reported a dream in which pus was coming out of his mother's breast. He abruptly ended his treatment when the therapist attempted such an interpretation. We can speculate that, had he continued his therapy, this dream would eventually come to be understood as a metaphor for his core relationship problem and would emerge as a resistance to a dependent transference (which is a form of transference resistance) as a defense against the toxicity he would attribute to the therapist.

THE CORE RELATIONSHIP PROBLEM
REENACTED WITH THE THERAPIST

Of the dynamics of transference, Freud (1912) says that, in analysis, there is a tendency toward the activation of unconscious fantasy, and that this process is a regressive one that revives the subject's infantile imagoes (102). He adds that when a person's need for love is not entirely satisfied by reality, that person tends to approach every new person he meets with anticipatory ideas, and that these are directed toward the analyst. He comments that "this cathexis will have recourse to prototypes, will attach itself to one of the stereotype plates which are present in the subject" (100).

The analogy of stereotype plates lends itself well to the concept of self- and object representations as structure, and the manner in which these representations are played out analogously to Freud's stereotype plates in the treatment situation. To the extent that the patient, for one reason or another, must cling to this stereotypical manner of relating, the transference will be a powerful source of resistance.

In their research of treatment outcomes, Luborsky (1988) and his colleagues found that patients benefit most when the therapist correctly identifies their core relationship problem *regardless of the presenting problem.* This means that we also cannot be boxed within the medical frame of

DSM4 terminology. Although those diagnoses are required on insurance forms, people do not fit neatly into categories. While categorical thinking provides the therapist with a false security of prepackaged certainty, it will lead to a serious inability to understand the person. I regularly hear therapists jump to diagnostic conclusions based on the presenting problem. A man troubled by his compulsive crossdressing made it clear that his desire was toward women. Gradually, it became clear that his core relationship conflict revolved around his mother's need to keep him dependent on her and her wish that he had been a girl. He grew up terrified of losing her and made the necessary adaptations that would ensure her continuing attachment to him. The core relationship problem entailed the many aspects of individuation that were blocked by his mother and were to become the focus of treatment. His problem had nothing to do with sex, although it was played out in the sexual arena. He did not have a gender identity disorder and his symptom had nothing to do with his sexual orientation. The symptom had to do with the potential anxiety and depression of object loss—the price he would have to pay for being a man—and his desperate attempts to reconstitute the lost connection with his mother by dressing as a female.

Inevitably, the patient attributed to the therapist the same maternal demand that he adapt to her needs and wishes, whatever he imagined they might be. This, also inevitably, became a point of impasse in the treatment, a transference resistance that had to be recognized and confronted by the therapist before the impasse could even begin to be dissolved. So long as the therapist saw the patient's presenting problem in sexual terms, all interventions were focused around these issues. The therapist did not recognize the mother–son relationship as the core of the patient's issues, and as such this became the heart of the treatment impasse.

Individual's core relationship problems are set up in the early, most formative years with the primary caretaker(s). Many therapists tend to become embroiled with the patient in marital or work problems; that is, they try to work in the derivatives of the developmental conflicts, neglecting how the individual came to this way of being in the world in the first place. They do not address the deeper, underlying unconscious wishes, fears, interpersonal dilemmas, and defenses that are acted out and manifest in the here-and-now situation. I liken this approach to looking in a mirror, seeing that you have dirt on your nose, then taking a tissue and trying to wipe the reflection in the mirror clean. Many therapies fail because of this approach.

THE CORE RELATIONSHIP
PROBLEM AS ORGANIZING PRINCIPLE

When we can identify the core relationship problem early in treatment, it becomes the *organizing principle* for understanding the later derivatives and the many layers of adaptive, expressive, or defensive elaboration that have accrued over the years. The core problem may involve issues around attachment, dependency, individuation, and autonomy, and the ways in which they have become convoluted, double-binding, or mystifying—leading to a variety of developmental pathologies and defenses. They may be imbued with issues of pride and shame, or eroticized within complex compromise formations. These complexities gradually reveal themselves in the work if we keep in mind the core issue and how new material is, to a greater or lesser degree, understandable from this perspective. Both therapist and patient come to see how it all makes sense. I am troubled by the current tendency in the field to give to many of these complexities a diagnosis, creating one disease entity after another with no recognition of where it fits into the whole picture of the person. Techniques to work with these so-called disorders spring up just as rapidly.

For example, as a powerful biological drive, sex has the ability to "capture" early unarticulated *relational* conflicts. The eroticization of the psychological conflict embedded in the compromise formation of sexual fantasy or perversion creates a psyche–soma link that further contributes to the power of this solution. Exploring masturbatory fantasies, although often uncomfortable for the therapist, can open up a rich and complex compromise formation. This inquiry entails asking who does what to whom. If the therapist avoids this exploration because of his or her own discomfort, the countertransference interferes with the work. Oedipal issues can become condensed into the core dynamic. Divested of the *sexual vehicle by means of which a relationship dynamic is expressed*—such as submission and domination—the core relationship problem and its complex consequences can be explored. Being the victim in a sadomasochistic fantasy affords the person the illusion of power and control over being hurt because, after all, he can start and stop the action when and how he pleases. The illusion of mastery over traumatic helplessness is temporarily soothing and reassuring, along with the gratification of sexual release. These psychological rewards reinforce the pathological solution, making it difficult to give up.

The core relationship problem embedded in the masturbatory fantasy will be expressed in the transference. As such, it will be the basis for a major transference resistance to change. The transference issue might long remain unrecognized by the therapist—even for years. However, once the interpersonal dynamic is extracted from the fantasy, the therapist can wonder both to himself and to the patient if the same dynamic isn't being played out with him or her in the therapeutic relationship.

Compromise formations may be embedded in a variety of fantasies, symptoms, or behaviors. As we decipher them *in relational terms,* we may be able to discover the elements of wish and fear, adaptation and defense, all woven together into a single fantasy or behavior. A relational pattern may both connect and disconnect, revealing the wish to connect, the fear of connecting, and the defense against what is feared. This may bring to mind the symptom of bulimia. While the compromise formation is a solution, it is not a resolution. In the instance of the connect/disconnect pattern, we will wonder, in developmental terms, about the wish that brings the individual toward the other and the rapidly ensuing fear of closeness that motivates his protective, distancing strategies. In interpersonal terms, what is the danger? Surely those issues will pertain to his therapist, often leading to a pattern of approach and avoidance that the therapist may come to feel frustrating and aggravating. This is a major transference (and countertransference) knot that must be recognized and dealt with therapeutically. Too often, the therapist in this situation will act out in a way that may not only jeopardize the treatment, but may also end it precipitously.

THE IMPORTANCE OF PRESERVING A PSYCHOLOGY OF THE MIND: OCD OR DEFENSE MECHANISM?

In his work on the "obsessive personality," Leon Saltzman (1968) refers to the obsessive defense and how it provides a feeling of security in a world in which uncertainty is inevitable. He observed that as a "style," obsessional patterns range *all the way from normal to psychotic.*

It is for this very reason that there is high potential for diagnostic and, thus, treatment errors when the therapist rushes to label the patient OCD without any idea of the underlying character structure or object relations set-up. Is the patient neurotic or is she borderline? One cannot help but wonder if such quick recourse to a medical explanation coupled with medical (psychopharmacological) treatment is not a manifestation of a countertransference resistance of a therapist who—to put it simply—does not know what else to do.

Recent advances in technology have opened up the brain to neurological researchers. Unfortunately, these discoveries have been used in the denial of intrapsychic and interpersonal conflicts. One does not see an individual with conflict, anxiety, and defense; one sees a sick patient with a disease that requires medical intervention.

The obsession, like a magnet, draws all attention, cognitive and emotional, away from where the conflict lies, focusing it elsewhere and providing a magical solution to the unresolved conflict or conflicts. Of course, this does not fix the problem because the solution is an illusion, a displacement, and offers only temporary respite from the distresses associated with the core conflict—thus the need to return to the solution again and again and the formation of an obsession.

We read about the findings of "junk science" (Milloy 2001), which sets out to prove a variety of preformed conclusions. Our culture flails about, alternating between a denial of what is psychological so as not to have to deal with it, and the elevation of junk science to the front page. Junk science is very poorly designed psychological and sociological "research" that is ultimately used to justify the preexisting attitudes of the researchers, to prove the point they want to make. The study is slanted to support and rationalize their own choices and decisions. They do not apply the basic principles of good research design. Other factors that are operating are not taken into account. These researchers assume that their interpretation of the findings is correct when many other interpretations may be equally plausible. When this happens, science itself must be called into question. Legitimate science does not have a vested interest in the outcome. What is sought is truth.

Because certain brain changes were observed in patients diagnosed as having an obsessive-compulsive disorder, a causal link has been stated, asserting that these changes cause the disorder. Anyone with any sophistication in statistical analysis knows that the cause–effect link—if there is indeed one—could just as well go in the other direction: that is, the obsessional disorder and the affective components central to a serious interpersonal, relational problem may cause these changes in the brain. We are all familiar with the changes that take place in our body when we are frightened. We are also familiar with the way in which mental activity of the mind affects the brain, as seen in the creation of visual images in dreams, even though the eyes are closed. The mind bypasses the sensory receptors and operates on the brain. There is even a third explanation of the research findings: that there is no causal link either way, but that both factors co-vary through a connection with a third factor. The statistical device, analysis of variance, or analysis of covariance attempts to answer such scientific questions.

An obsessional disorder is one manifestation of a compromise formation. If we can resist the dazzle of the medical perspective and what is designated "OCD" and return to a psychological perspective—to a psychology of the mind—we will once again view the obsession not as a "sickness," but as a defense mechanism. And as we all know, the obsessional defense creates another level of distress, such as shame about having it. Sexual obsessions fit in this category, as do eating obsessions. I do not use the term "eating disorder," which gives it medical stand-alone status. I see the various "eating disorders" as manifestations of the obsessional defense against the conflict inherent in the core relational problem.

Along with the direct interpretation of the defensive function of the obsession, a formulation is made of the *interpersonal* nature of the core conflict that is relevant to the specifics of the individual's developmental history and internal object relations. For example, hypochondriacal fears that the body may turn against itself in the form of cancer or some other life-threatening illness may be seen in some cases as a defense against the recognition and acknowledgment of mother's hatred or hostility. Such a recognition is so unbearable and so frightening that premature or overly aggressive interpretation may lead to a flight from treatment. At the same time, the patient pleads for relief. The therapist may be between a rock and a hard place and be tempted to refer the patient for medication as a way out of his or her own distress. The development of pain in one woman's breast whenever something good happened could be understood as a somatic response to her mother's envious hatred and her fear of an attack by her mother. McDougall (1974) noted that "the body lends itself and its functions to the mind to use as the mind wills." In the course of therapy, the emergence of awareness of the hatred by and toward the mother may be accompanied by a stormy hypochondriacal obsession and symptoms.

Smoking often takes on an obsessional quality, perhaps being labeled an addiction—another "disease" category. Whatever the physiologically addictive qualities of nicotine may be, it is the psychological dynamic that has a hold on the individual. I have found in such cases that the person in question long ago submitted to the relationship rule that she has no right to have a wish or desire of her own, and that if she does express one, the narcissistic mother will be enraged. The patient's role has been to fit herself into the other's psychological drama and scenario, to tend to mother's wishes and desires. This has become the patient's way of being in the world in general and with the therapist in particular. With all other avenues of desire blocked, now by the internalized forbidding mother, desire discovers an outlet. She can have what she wants when she wants it—the cigarette. There is an illusion of control. We might even perceive a tantrum quality to that insistence.

FROM OBJECT RELATIONS TO THE DYNAMICS OF INTERPERSONAL RELATIONSHIPS

This approach is a further elaboration of my own object relations orientation. Each stage along the developmental line—from birth, attachment, separation and individuation, and later development in childhood and adolescence—has its own developmental tasks and stage-specific and appropriate requirements of the caretaking environment. Each stage has its own pitfalls, where significant failure of that environment will leave lasting effects on the character structure and on the manner in which the individual connects with others and relates to them in an ongoing way. *That is, structural pathology and relational conflict can arise at any of these stages along the developmental continuum.* When we are able to understand where the point of derailment occurred, we can get a clearer picture of both the strengths and vulnerabilities of the individual. For example, if the first three years went well, but then things went wrong when the child tried to move away from her mother toward her father, and then to friends, we can rely on the psychological solidity that comes with a good first three years. We can rely on the presence of a cohesive self and a degree of mental individuation in the therapy. We can interpret conflict, anxiety, and defense and not have to walk on eggs, lest we evoke a paranoid reaction or loss of self-cohesion.

Object relations theory focuses on the intrapsychic structure that evolves within the earliest interpersonal relationships and plays a central role in the interpersonal relationships in adult life. In *Working with the Core Relationship Problem in Psychotherapy* (Horner 1998), I shifted my emphasis from what is structural to what is dynamically relational. Taking the same approach here, I am focusing on the psychodynamic expression of the underlying character structure.

The term "object relations" is a structural concept referring to inner mental structures of the self and object representations and their dynamic interplay as well as the characteristic feelings, wishes, and fears of this setup. The object-relational situation—the inner psychological structure—becomes manifest in interpersonal relationships, with transference of particular interest to the therapist. The term "relational" can be used to describe the interpersonal aspect of whatever theory a particular writer espouses. That is, *it is generic* and cannot be claimed by any given theoretical school, although it may be more or less central depending on the theoretical approach.

TRANSFERENCE RESISTANCE

"Resistance" is an unfortunate term for the manifestation of defense mechanisms or character defenses in the treatment situation. Using the word with a psychoanalytically unsophisticated patient may evoke undesired consequences because, to the patient, it implies deliberate intent and thus, blame. From the patient's unconscious, or at times conscious, point of view, these defenses protect the self from a variety of intrapsychic or interpersonal dangers. These dangers often go together in the patient's mind. For example, fear of losing control of one's hostile aggression may elicit fear of loss of the hated but needed object. As long as these defenses are in play, the process of exploration and discovery comes to a halt. They must be understood and their important functions carefully analyzed. In addition to articulating the danger behind the defense, it is necessary to articulate the unconscious wishes embedded in the resistance.

Resistances have been classified in different ways over the years, often depending on the author's theoretical orientation. For example, Freud (1926) used three major terms, ego-resistance, id-resistance, and super-ego-resistance. Greenson (1967) summarized the situation, saying that the underlying theme is that resistance analysis (and, particularly, transference resistance analysis) comprises the heart and soul of psychoanalytic treatment.

The core relationship problem will be manifest in the transference, in the subtle and not-so-subtle ways in which the patient relates to the therapist. The therapist has to be sensitive and tuned into these nuances. The term "transference resistence" refers to a defensive mode of relating to the therapist. It can be viewed as the patient's way of *managing* the therapeutic relationship in such a manner as to bring about a wished-for kind of interaction or prevent a form of interaction that is a feared source of anxiety. It may come out of anxiety due to neurotic conflict. It may also be based on the dictates of character pathology. This set-up often causes treatment impasses because the therapist, unaware of this process, may unconsciously collude with the patient.

One example is a patient's chronic helpless complaining, which presents the therapist with a felt implicit demand that she fix the problem. This, of course, stirs up difficult feelings in the therapist, particularly a sense of helplessness. One could speculate that, as a child, the patient was assigned the impossible task of trying to cure or cheer up his sickly, complaining, or depressed mother. Family therapist James Framo (1970) referred to such situations as "irrational role assignment." What the therapist feels now may reveal what it felt like to be that child. Going through the therapist's mind may be an irritable, "Well, what do you expect *me* to do about it?" Analysts will recognize the process of projective identification in this example. The patient reenacts his mother's complaining stance and the therapist experiences what it was like for that child to have that mother. Despite the irritation, if the therapist is able to understand what is taking place, she can use the information as a source of empathy for the child the patient once was. The therapist can then soften her confrontation of the patient's acting-out resistance with this newfound empathy.

Another example is a stance of pleasing or entertaining the therapist. A countertransference-based collusion may occur when the therapist rather likes the break from the tension of a day of seeing difficult patients. This one is a relief!

Friedman (1997) refers to what he calls the "demand structure of treatment." He adds, "If you don't offer one demand, the patient will perceive another." Like it or not, the therapist will carry the psychological weight of an authority figure, a powerful parental object—at least at the level of the patient's unconscious. The perceived demand will derive from conscious or unconscious beliefs and expectations inherent in the core relationship problem. An example of such an assumed demand is that he, the patient, must be responsive to the narcissistic vulnerabilities that are transferentially attributed to you, the therapist. As with his mother, he must never upset you. Your love must be bought at a price to the self. He will relate to you in adaptation to these attributed demands.

One therapist noticed that she and the patient frequently would start to say something at the same time. He would always politely tell her to go ahead. When it became clear that this was a pattern in which a relationship rule was being played out—he must always submit to the will of his mother—the therapist was able to comment on it. The transaction knot disappeared and the patient's self-defeating ways of relating to others were further illuminated.

When a therapist abandons his position of neutrality in the service of being "encouraging" or "supportive," the patient may experience this as a demand for improvement. Whether she overtly complies or passive-aggressively, covertly defies, a transference resistance is the outcome. When the therapist actively supports the patient as she complains about the behavior or failings of a friend or lover, the patient's internal conflict becomes externalized and is played out with the therapist. The therapist has now become the proxy for the patient's negativity toward that other person. "But I love him!" will be the unexpected protest.

Attending to this transference resistance gives direct information about the wishes and fears associated with the core relationship conflicts. It also provides information with respect to the adaptations and defenses that evolved over the years and that now cause problems in and of themselves. That is, they are maladaptive even though they may have felt necessary to the survival of the self at one time. In my many years of experience as a consultant, transference resistance more often then not was central to the treatment impasse. In most such cases, the situation was made worse by the therapist's conscious or unconscious collusion.

For example, a patient who was required to be dumb in order to puff up her mother's self-esteem and a therapist who has a need to know all the answers will connect like two pieces of Velcro, resulting in a misalliance where transference resistance meets countertransference resistance. Paying attention to the transference–countertransference mix usually reveals the core relationship problem in action.

Does the person alternate between intense attempts to connect either through seduction, ingratiation, or self-effacing servitude and *flight away* from the relationship in order to reconnect with the self? A history of an in-and-out pattern in therapy may indicate the existence of this double approach–avoidance conflict. To connect with the other is to lose the self. To connect with the self is to lose the other (Horner 1999). This kind of vacillation in and out of a relationship, including the therapeutic relationship, will characterize this person's way of being in the world. It is a lose-lose set-up leading to a sense of hopelessness that relationships may never work out. Sexual acting out can be a compromise formation that connects and disconnects at the same time.

Once we have ascertained the core relationship problem as it is manifest in the treatment relationship, it is important that it be laid out in a manner that communicates empathy with the individual's dilemma as he or she was growing up—with an understanding of how it came to be in the first place, perhaps in the service of emotional survival. In the interest of so-called empathy, we must be careful not to "validate" or "normalize" the patient's present-day maladaptive behaviors and the feelings behind them in such a way as to remove them from consideration as a source of the individual's unhappiness. Horney (1945) emphasizes this, saying:

> Resistance toward recognizing the consequences of neurotic attitudes and drives is for the most part deeply concealed and may be easily overlooked by the analyst for the very reason that to him the connection is so obvious. This is unfortunate, because unless the patient is made aware that he blinds himself to consequences and the reasons for which he does so, he cannot possibly realize to what an extent he interferes with his own life. Awareness of consequences is the most powerful curative factor in analysis in that it impresses on the patient's mind that only by changing certain things within himself can he ever attain freedom.

The therapist walks a narrow line between protecting the patient from such awareness and sounding to the patient like he is being told that his unhappiness is all his own fault. This is where empathic understanding of the *child's* dilemma and limited power helps ameliorate such a potentially blaming stance on the part of the therapist. The sooner the core relationship conflict is interpreted, the less likely there will be an acting-out against the therapist and against the therapy.

We also find resistance to the work itself, although the therapist will certainly be seen as the agent of the work and thus dangerous in her own right. The work may endanger something that must be preserved—regardless of how problematic it may be—and a self-destruct mechanism is activated by that threat to the individual's uneasy homeostasis within the core relationship conflict.

A not uncommon clinical issue is the individual's quasi-symbiotic tie to his mother. We may, in our therapeutic zeal, see helping him "separate and individuate" as the goal of treatment. I once heard this referred to as "wedge therapy." Jeopardy to the patient's connection with his object will make it necessary for him to block any treatment he experiences as aimed at breaking his bond/bind with his mother. The therapist's understanding and articulation of the core relationship conflict, the inevitable ambivalence toward connection, and the wish–fear dilemma all make it more likely to prevent an acting-out against the treatment itself. I find it useful to articulate the dilemma the patient is in, caught in a kind of triangle between his mother, his therapist, and the therapy. The therapist is caught in the same dilemma—often finding herself damned if she does and damned if she doesn't. Articulating this shared condition reveals the degree to which the patient's adaptations and defensive strategies cause others pain, and makes it clear that he is not a victim. As it is, if he and the therapist define the goal of treatment as his becoming more autonomous, he will not only be disloyal to his mother; he might even be responsible for her failure to thrive. His "recovery" may mean her destruction. The strength of the dangerous anger and aggression that must be repressed will most likely be in proportion to the felt sense of paralysis resulting from the core relationship conflict. These patients will probably be found to have been derailed from the developmental continuum at the stage of individuation.

CHARACTER RESISTANCE

Far more malignant situations where attachment from the very start has been compromised by any of a variety of serious psychological factors or physical abuses are a different story. Sandler (1990) notes that "one source of severe resistance in analysis, which often leads to a negative therapeutic reaction, is our need to cling to the internal objects we have constructed" (878–79). The negative therapeutic reaction refers to those situations in which the analytic work itself, particularly if apparently successful, creates anxiety, depression, or some other manifestation of loss of progress. One woman noted that if she gave up her pathological tie to her mother, who used the daughter as a receptacle for her projective identifications, she would have nothing but blackness and emptiness. Patients with a paranoid core cling to their persecutory objects, inner and outer, as a way to defend themselves against falling into the "black hole" (Grotstein 1990), the empty despair of an anaclitic depression. In situations like these, we come up against not only transference resistances manifesting the core relationship problem, but more pervasive, characterological resistances that protect a fragile or tenuous structure.

Kohut (1971) makes a similar distinction. He speaks of *nonspecific* resistances, as treatment as a whole offends the patient's pride by contradicting his fantasies of omnipotence and self-sufficiency by which he maintains his self-cohesion. In contrast, there are *specific* resistances against the dangers of opening himself up to his therapist, anticipating fearful reenactments of early childhood relationship frustrations, disappointments, and thus conflict with the therapist.

Krystal (1978) describes psychic trauma as the outcome of being confronted with *overwhelming* affect. In this situation, the "affective responses produce an unbearable psychic state which threatens to disorganize, perhaps even destroy all psychic functions" (82). Khan (1963) referred to *cumulative trauma,* which results when the primary caretaker fails to function adequately as a protective shield for the baby. A nonempathic and nonresponsive mother is not the only problem that may cause such trauma. The child may be ill and in pain, so that the mother is powerless to alleviate it, no matter how hard she tries. Whatever the reason, the child is subjected to repeated traumatic states that interfere with the synthesization of a cohesive self. Krystal notes that, in adult life, the fear of affect may represent the dread of returning to this infantile trauma. Pervasive defenses against this feared state will lead to a form of resistance that will be seen as more characterological than transferential.

It is still possible to work with this resistance against affect cognitively. Winnicott (1974) views the fear of breakdown as a fear that something will happen that has *already* happened. I find it useful to interpret this fear, and also the temporary states of being overwhelmed, as a *memory,* a total recall of something that cannot be remembered in any other way because it never was symbolized by language. Not only does this interpretation separate past from present, but it also makes an important distinction between the relative helplessness of the baby and the resources that the individual now has as an adult. The emergence of the traumatic state no longer signifies to the patient that he or she is "crazy" or hopelessly mentally ill. At this point the transference resistance can be addressed, noting its connection to the fear of the dreaded traumatic state. Issues of trust are most likely to be prominent. Will the therapist be more reliable than the failed mother of infancy? Character resistances may often protect the patient from feared transference enactments as well.

These all-pervasive character defenses emerge as *character resistances* in treatment. These are the treatments in which the therapist may function as a "new object" or provide a "holding environment" (Winnicott 1971) for a prolonged initial period of work. Aspects of the more specific, clearly object-related transferences that emerge as points of impasse in the treatment are the *transference resistances.*

CORE PROBLEM INDICATORS

The core relationship problem will be revealed in many ways. Asking for the patient's earliest memory may give us insight into what appear to be here-and-now anxieties of a specific kind. Remembering the terror of being lost in a department store at the age of three may relate to the panic felt when driving in unfamiliar locations, where the fear of getting lost is incompatible with the characteristic high level of functioning in other emergency situations. Despite the anxiety, there is a cohesive self and the patient can tolerate the anxiety of working interpretively. The metaphor of being lost will help unravel later emotional elaborations of the fear and the defenses against it. Perhaps getting lost (cut off from her object) will be the consequence of moving toward autonomy.

In another instance, the patient's earliest memory, one from the age of three, was of having his mother scold him when their new puppy bit him. This memory became a signifier for his mother's characteristic failures of empathy.

End of the hour comments from the patient such as "There's never enough time" may signify, for example, a mother who could not tolerate the temporary regression of her child's refueling attempts during the rapprochement period or, even after that, a mother who demanded a self-sufficiency of which the child was not yet capable. The core relationship conflict will develop around the need to perform—to be a good girl—with a denial of dependency wishes and an avoidance of that aspect of the transference and the analytic work. To complicate the scenario, shame becomes associated with the baby self and pride with the ability to perform. Shame–pride issues often complicate relational conflict. Sometimes this developmental background becomes manifest in what is referred to as a "resistance to a dependent transference," a particular variety of transference resistance.

Careful listening and judicious inquiry in the intake interview may lead to clues as to the core relationship problem, how it arose, and what the psychological consequences have been throughout life. For example, in her first session, a woman commented on her terrible guilt. I asked, "So what's your crime?" Without hesitation she replied, "To have a self." These four words opened up the exploration of both inner and interpersonal consequences of having been abused emotionally and physically with a constant assault on anything that might be deemed expressive of self. If she failed to hide her feelings, she felt the back of her father's hand. If she expressed her thoughts, she was told she was crazy. If she expressed wish or need, she was told she was selfish.

Bromberg (1996) notes that *we do not try to cure people of what happened to them. We try to cure them of what they now do to themselves and others in order to cope with what happened to them.* From these maladaptive patterns of life, we will be able to pull out underlying wishes and fears with respect to relationships.

The initial negotiation of the therapy arrangement is also likely to be shaped by the core relationship problem. Issues of the frequency of meetings as well as the fees will also be rich in clinically relevant information. If the patient only wants to come in once a week but submits to the therapist's insistence that sessions must be more frequent in order for the work to be productive, the therapist may find that he or she has inadvertently activated a core conflict characterized by a pattern of overt compliance and covert defiance, which simultaneously connects to and distances from the other. There is a wish *and* a fear with respect to intimate relationships. It is important that a power struggle not be set up at the outset, although it would be premature to interpret the dynamic. If the therapy goes well, this individual is likely to bring up the issue of a second session herself. The desire will be *hers,* not the therapist's to which she must acquiesce.

BELIEFS AND THE UNCONSCIOUS: UNCONSCIOUS BASIC PREMISES REGARDING INTERPERSONAL RELATIONSHIPS

The core relationship problem will also be manifest in a person's belief system—the basic assumptions and premises on which all reasoning is based (Horner 1997). As the child develops within the relational matrix with his mother and father, as well as within his wider family system as a whole, he builds up a system of beliefs about himself, about others, and about the nature of human relationships. These belief systems are set up early in childhood and come out of a combination of what is experienced vis-à-vis the environment and the limited thinking and reasoning of which the child is capable as he tries to make sense of his universe. In circular fashion, just as early experience generates belief systems, belief systems shape and define current experience. Some of these beliefs entail:

1. What I have to do or be like in order to connect with the other.
2. What I have to do or be like to be safe.
3. What I have to do or be like to be secure in a relationship.
4. What I have to do or be like to feel good about myself.
5. What I have to do or be like to have my wishes come true.
6. What I have to do or be like to be sure my fears do *not* come true.

Exploring the core relational problem entails an exploration of the belief system as part of that process. Present experiences and events continue to be assimilated into the preexisting belief and are interpreted as a validation of those beliefs. If he believes his wishes and desires are unreasonable, overwhelming the other and driving her away, any disappointment in an interaction will be explained to the self as the result of this dynamic. "She didn't want to see me anymore because I was just too much for her." The perceived negative maternal attitude toward his little-boy needs and desires came to define him—he was "someone who was too much."

When his little brother was born, a man who was the oldest of four children and who had a benign and healthy relationship with his mother up to that event, wondered to himself, "Why wasn't I enough?" From then on, his way of being with his mother and later with others was to endeavor to be "enough," whatever he imagined that to be. Any disappointments in his relationships would be interpreted as the result of his not being enough. Such assumptions act like a magnet, drawing present conflict into their orbit, serving as an explanation for present relationship conflicts. In her paper, "How the Brain Actively Constructs Perceptions," Pally (1997) says that the implication of the neurological underpinning of perception is "not so much that people . . . repeat the same experience but that they tend to interpret current situations with a bias toward what has occurred in the past."

The core relationship problem is essentially the scaffold around which subsequent development is organized. It has complex paths leading from it in many directions. Construction of the developmental hypothesis is not the end of the work; it is the start. The therapist has to be something of a novelist, to put together the person's story (read "history" as "his story") from a wide variety of informative verbal and behavioral communications by the patient. The story provides a matrix within which the patient can be better understood in the here-and-now, so that ultimately everything that happens in the course of treatment makes sense. That which the patient fears is "crazy" can come to be seen as understandable under the circumstances. That alone relieves the individual of shame and anxiety about his or her life, about who he or she is in the world today.

The next chapter develops the concept of the developmental continuum and the consequences of psychological derailment at any point along that continuum.

1

The Core Relationship Problem as Resistance

THE DEVELOPMENTAL CONTINUUM

The following diagram taken from *Object Relations and the Developing Ego in Therapy* (Horner 1979, 1984) is included here to clarify what is meant by the "developmental continuum." For purposes of this book, it would have to be extended through later childhood and adolescence, inasmuch as derailment is possible at those periods as well. The diagram helps conceptualize what is meant by "derailment" and see what developmental tasks have been foreclosed by it.

DEVELOPMENTAL TASKS

Successful negotiation of the developmental tasks associated with these early years leads to the *formation of a cohesive, reality-related, object-related self.*

The cohesive self is characterized by an adequate integration of affect, impulse, perception, and cognition. It is not subject to self-dissolution, fragmentation, or disorganization. Interpersonal relationships are not characterized by splitting. Winnicott (1965) writes about the importance of a sense of "going-on-being." This sense fails in the presence of dissociated self-states (Horner 1999). A serious failure of the caretaking environment to provide a stable and predictable interpersonal matrix within which the organization of the nascent self can proceed relatively free from disruption leads to such a situation. The development of children

Stages and Processes in the Development of Early Object Relations and Their
Associated Pathologies (Horner 1979, 1984)

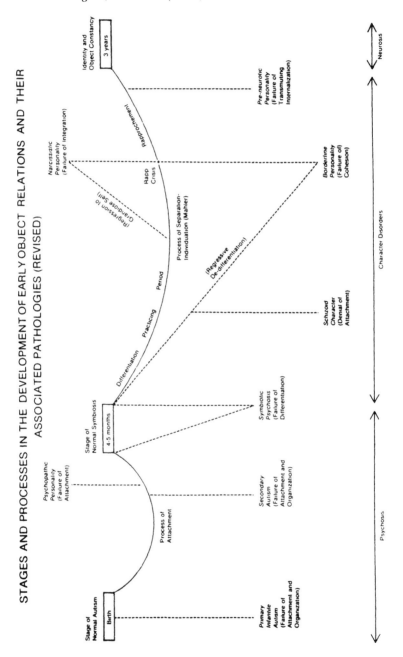

who grow up in institutions or who are sent from pillar to post in a series of foster home placements is compromised from the start.

The self develops within the context of the maternal matrix, and the primary mothering person is viewed as the mediator of organization. The consistent and predictable presence of the good-enough mother throughout the early months of life serves to tie the infant's universe of experience together in a particular way. First of all, she prevents the traumatic emotional states that overwhelm the nascent ego structure and impede organization. Then, it is through her that the body, impulse, feeling, action, and eventually thought become organized as part of the self and integrated not only with one another, but also with the external reality of which she is a representative. The mothering person not only mediates this process of organization and reality-relatedness, but her image as manifest in the nature of characteristic interactions is also part of what is organized and is the basis for the development of object relatedness as well. Indeed, one might say that *the mother is the linchpin of the psyche.*

Discontinuity in the child's experience of who the mother is due to her character pathology leads to a discontinuity in the experience of the self in relation to her as well. These different states cannot be integrated. A cohesive self cannot be consolidated. From the patient's point of view, the existence of these dissociated self-states is particularly disruptive. *When any one self-state is present, the experience takes on a totality; it is all that is available to consciousness and is all that feels real.* Emotional and cognitive strengths and resources that are characteristic of a relatively positive state will be unremembered and unavailable when the person is in a state of catastrophic emergency.

We can best understand the self-states from a relationship—or interpersonal—perspective. That is, *each separate self has its own connection with an aspect of the primary object and bears its own imprint of affect and thought.* When the patient, as a result of the work of therapy, gradually becomes aware and conscious of the coexistence of the several dissociated states, and that they may even coexist in some dynamic relation to one another, the beginning of integration is under way. A direct link is made between each state and a corresponding experience of the mother in the formative years. A mother who herself manifests dissociated self-states leaves the child little option but to *adapt* to each of the mothers presented to him. When attempts are made to reconcile the irreconcilable, as they must, dissociation is a way out, a way to reduce cognitive dissonance or unbearable conflict. The task of integration is as much cognitive as it is emotional, if not more so.

As the core relationship problem, these states will become manifest in treatment with disparate transference issues that parallel the disparity in the self. The work of cognitive integration is necessary before direct work on the transference can be undertaken. The dissociation is, in effect, the character resistance.

In a more evolved character structure—under the impact of intrapsychic conflict—integrated feelings, wishes, or thoughts may be subject to repression. However, their reemergence into consciousness will result in guilt or anxiety—and not in disorganization. When there are deficits in cohesion, the individual is excessively dependent on the object. Differentiation and object loss result in a loss of cohesion and dissolution of the self. In psychotherapy, the individual will strive to protect his connection with the therapist. Transference resistance will have, as its motive, the sense that survival depends on maintaining that connection. There will also be character resistances to those thoughts, affects, or impulses that threaten the cohesion of the self.

The reality-related self not only has adequate reality testing. There is also a firm sense of a real self in contact with the external world, and particularly with the interpersonal environment. An example of the failure to achieve a reality-related self is what is described by Winnicott (1965) as the False Self. The True Self is split off and repressed. These patients often report dreams of buried babies. One man dreamed of a grandmotherly figure helping him dig up a buried baby—a positive transference dream, to be sure. The false self is consolidated around the child's adaptation to the other. The true-self identity is consolidated around that which originates from within and to which the object responds empathically. A self that is cut off from reality-relatedness and is in quasi-autistic isolation is potentially a delusional self.

When the false self is brought into the therapeutic alliance, what appears to be a therapeutic process is, in fact, an acting out. As such, it is a transference resistance. To the extent that the therapist participates in the alliance with the false self, he is either consciously or unconsciously in collusion with the resistance. This would be his countertransference resistance.

The object-related self is characterized by internalizations and identifications that, in optimum development, lead to libidinal object constancy; to a well-secured identity with the capacity to regulate one's narcissistic equilibrium from resources within the self; to the capacity for signal anxiety; and finally, to the structuring of the superego. Failure to achieve this degree of structural maturity may lead to the setting up of maladaptive dependent relationships, which often are reflective of the core relationship problem. They are apt to be reenacted in the therapy relationship as well. This reenactment will stand as a powerful transference resistance.

Detachment and denial of the significance of the therapist as a person constitutes a transference resistance. What is being defended against is a reenactment of a pathological relationship, the loss of a separate self, or the dangers of overwhelming negative affect. The use of schizoid defenses may make possible success in the world of work. Whether a college professor or a bank president, it is the nonrelatedness that makes these achievements possible. The pathology of the split-off self will only become evident when the person finds himself in a more intimate situation. Of course, this will be true of psychotherapy.

The developmental tasks of later childhood and adolescence take place outside the family and its primary relationships. The child begins to develop interests, skills, and abilities. At this stage, school and teachers become more important. The child also has to learn to get along with other children. The child with significant narcissistic vulnerabilities and defenses does not fare well in a community of his peers.

The specific developmental tasks of adolescents are: (1) to come to terms with bodily changes and emerging sexual feelings and make them part of the self, (2) to develop a set of values to live by, (3) to achieve independence from parents, (4) to establish peer-group relations with members of both sexes, and (5) to make a vocational choice or set further educational goals toward making such a choice. The new demands made on the young person will be affected by his or her ability to relate to others in a caring way rather than out of need, a clear sense of self or identity, and the self-confidence and ability to think and act independently. Tasks of both later childhood and adolescence are likely to be foreclosed as the result of early developmental derailment. The not uncommon breakdown of the boy or girl upon leaving home for college is an example of the deleterious impact of an underlying pathology of character structure.

STAGES OF DEVELOPMENT

Particularly relevant to this perspective is the work of Mahler (1968; Mahler, Pine, and Bergman 1975), as well as that of Bowlby (1969), Winnicott (1965), and Kohut (1971). Each of these developmental stages, which are defined in terms of the nature of the self- and object representations and their relationship to one another, leaves its traces in the unconscious. Even in the fully evolved individual, they may be reactivated under stress and regression, or in dream and fantasy. However, they are not likely to be acted out in reality. If they are, they are readily amenable to interpretation.

Preattachment

At birth, despite the immediate activation of the process of attachment, there is as yet no enduring, structured internal mental representations of self or object. Although the precursors of these representations are present in terms of an innate preference for patterns of a facial configuration over a geometric or other nonhuman-type pattern (Fantz 1966), along with readiness and potential for growth, the cognitive development that is necessary for the structuring of mental schemata and for the development of structure has not yet occurred. It is this *stage of preattachment* that may be activated in regressions that evoke an anaclitic depression, a feeling of a "black hole" or "nothingness" (Grotstein 1990). Character defenses and, hence, resistances, will stand between the patient and these dreadful experiences. Winnicott (1974) explains the fear of breakdown as the fear of something that has already happened. That is, these experiences of the adult patient are essentially memories of infantile experiences that can only be remembered in this way inasmuch as this experience was never symbolized or organized linguistically. They are not unlike the "flashback" of later traumatic events. Interpreting them as a memory makes the patient feel less "crazy" and more hopeful toward the outcome of therapy.

A woman had been told many times what a good baby she had been because she would wait patiently in her crib for long periods of time while her mother was busy. In therapy, she reported fears of "falling into the abyss." It became clear that this state could be activated in the present when she felt she had to "passively endure" distressing situations. Exploring this belief in terms of the core relationship problem, she was able to change that particular style of passive behavior and prevent the reexperience of the abyss.

Process of Attachment

The *process of attachment* takes place over the earliest months of life, leading to the early structure that includes the self, the primary caretaker, and *the salient qualities of their characteristic interaction.* It is here that the basis for an affectional relationship and what Erikson (1950) refers to as "basic trust" is laid down. It is also where basic distrust, or an internal world of persecutory objects, is laid down. There may also be disruptions of the attachment process due to illness, separation or loss, or unstable and inconsistent caretaking environments. The relevance of this to the present-day practice of placing infants or toddlers in a variety of day care situations is not to be underestimated. Therapists of the future will find themselves dealing with many of these children when they grow up. Current research on how well children do in day care may, in the long run, be seen as flawed. A child with an insecure attachment may do well in school in reading and math and seem to have no significant problems. She may have learned to adapt to the situation. But when that child becomes an adult, the inability to form lasting intimate relationships may be what brings her into psychotherapy.

At the most primitive level, failure of attachment may carry with it severe deficits in the early organization of the self. Bowlby (1946) described the "affectionless psychopath" as the case where there is a failure to develop the affectional bond that goes with attachment. Rutter (1974) described characteristic disturbances, such as an inability to keep rules, a lack of the capacity to experience guilt, and an indiscriminate friendliness with an inordinate craving for affection with no ability to make lasting friendships.

Bowlby (1960) notes that the persistent longing of the young child for the lost love object is often suffused with intense generalized hostility. He writes, "There is no experience to which a young child can be subjected that is more prone to elicit intense and violent hatred for the mother than that of separation" (24). He also notes that there is reason to believe that with prolonged and repeated separations during the first three years of life, a defensive detachment can persist indefinitely.

The patient with this kind of history may bring that defensive detachment into the treatment process where it will be manifest as a *resistance to a dependent transference.* This may be a form of either character resistance or transference resistance. That is, it may be pervasive and protect the character structure itself, or it may be more specific to the core relationship problem. The quality of the child's experience during the attachment process is built into his or her inner world of unconscious characteristic feelings and expectations about the interpersonal world, and this will color all later developmental stages and interpersonal relationships. This is where derailment and the setting up of the core relationship problem will take place. Wishes and fears associated with this core issue will lead to a variety of transference resistances.

Normal Stage of Symbiosis

Midway between the process of attachment and the separation–individuation process (Mahler 1968) stands the primitive mental structure, the undifferentiated selfobject representations. Owing to the infant's immature cognitive abilities, these images are organized on the basis of the predominant feelings that go with the interactions between self and other. The good self- and object images are linked by positive feelings and mood. The bad self- and object images are linked by negative feelings and mood. It is not until the end of the second year of life, with further cognitive development, that the disparate images will be integrated into single, albeit ambivalent, and separate images of self and other. If the good–bad split persists into adult life, it leads to an inability to form healthy and enduring relationships. When the other fails to be all good because of a failure to meet the wishes or demands of the self, he or she then becomes all bad and is discarded, or becomes the object of intense hatred.

No sooner is the symbiotic structure established intrapsychically than the child moves toward a new process, that of separation and individuation (Mahler, Pine, and Bergman 1975).

Process of Separation and Individuation

The overall *process of separation and individuation* takes place in stages marked by an increasing differentiation of the primitive self representation from that of the object representation. In the earlier part of this process, certain functions begin to emerge as a consequence of the maturation of the central nervous system, such as locomotion, perception, and learning. These are referred to as the *autonomous functions of the ego.* As the child feels the excitement of being able to stand alone and walk, he appears to be in an elated mood. This is the peak point of the child's belief in his or her own magic omnipotence. Mahler (1968) tells us that this is "still to a considerable degree derived *from* his sense of sharing in mother's magic powers" (20). This is the anlage of the grandiose observed in some adult patients.

The point of derailment from the developmental continuum establishes the degree to which this differentiation has been compromised. When the self representation remains intertwined with the object representation, the loss of the object and the sense of connection with that person may evoke a sense of disorganization and dissolution. When the unconscious psychic structure is dominated by this picture, the patient may experience severe separation panics. These separations can be due to the break in the emotional connection with the significant other just as much as to an actual physical separation. It is this sense of inner-connectedness that remains critical and that is so insecure. Transference resistances that protect the patient from such disruption of a dependent transference may include a false self adaptation, which may obscure the underlying core relationship problem and the anxieties attendant to it. On the other hand, along with anxious clinging, there may be a variety of strategies to capture and hold the object.

Rapprochement and the Rapprochement Crisis

The *rapprochement phase*, starting with *the rapprochement crisis*, marks the final step in separation and individuation. It is, perhaps, one of the most common places of developmental derailment found in patients who, at times, function reasonably well in the world. However, later on, important interpersonal relationships are marked by adaptations the child made to mother and father as a defense against the loss of those important connections.

At around the age of eighteen months, the toddler becomes increasingly aware of his or her separateness from mother and mother's separateness from him or her. Language begins to play an increasing role in interpersonal interaction and in the child's attempts to make sense of his experience. The child's experiences with reality have counteracted the more primitive overestimation of infantile omnipotence, self-esteem has been deflated, and the child is vulnerable to shame. This marks the so-called *rapprochement crisis.* Furthermore, through a now-conscious awareness of the need for the object, who is now perceived as powerful, the child is confronted with the relative helplessness of the self. There is an upsurge of separation anxiety and depressed mood. If the primary caretaker uses power in a benign and helpful manner, that power is the basis for the child's sense of security. If, on the other hand, parental power is experienced as against the self, as something that is not only given but withheld, the child comes to both hate and envy that power and will develop techniques to control it. This also may come to characterize the individual's relationship with his therapist. Behind such controlling behavior lies insecurity and anxiety. Therapists often have negative countertransference reactions to patients who manifest this pattern. Power struggles may develop with both countertransference resistance and transference resistance joining to bring the treatment to a standstill, if not to an abrupt end.

The major concern of the individual who struggles with issues associated primarily with this stage of development is the loss of support, love, and approval of the other that is feared to be a consequence of the assertion of one's own wishes or feelings or any other aspect of one's individuality. Still vulnerable to feelings of helplessness and shame, the person may tend to idealize the other and see the other as having the power to protect him from these painful feelings. This persisting dependent way of seeing the self and the other, and the expectations and demands that go with it, puts a strain on interpersonal relationships in general, and on the therapy relationship in particular. Although the other may be idealized, he or she is also envied, feared, and blamed when things do not go well. Kohut's (1971) work is especially relevant in this situation. The various narcissistic transferences described in *The Analysis of the Self* reflect the progressive and regressive stances of the patient toward the therapist. For example, he relates how a failure of the idealizing transference is followed by a devaluation of the therapist and a retreat to the grandiose self. The failure of the therapist to adequately navigate these stormy waters may provoke a further regression with a dissolution of the self or to an underlying paranoid structure.

When prior psychological development has not gone well, the conscious awareness of the realities of separateness and the loss of omnipotence may be very traumatic. If there are deficits in the structural organization of the self- and object representations, either as the result of unfavorable circumstance or as the result of some deficit in the child's synthesizing abilities, these deficits become evident at this time. The child, and the adult he or she becomes, is unable to negotiate the developmental demands. Symptomatic behavior such as anxious clinging often develops.

The term "rapprochement" suggests the alternating moving away from and then returning to mother for emotional refueling. Healthy parents do not have a need for the child either to stay dependent and helpless or to be completely self-reliant. The patient who brings a history of precocious independence and self-reliance will defend mightily against a dependent transference. Pride was associated with being "a big girl" and shame with being a "baby." These feelings play a major role in the patient's resistance to any manifestation of dependency, and he or she will defend against re-experiencing the cut-off, needy, and dependent child-self. The therapist must explore this dilemma, at the same time being careful not to shame the patient. In contrast, the patient who was required to stay a dependent child will resist the therapist's loss of neutrality when the therapist actively "supports" or advocates for healthy steps forward. Both sides of this coin are derived from the core relationship problem and become a resistance to change in therapy.

The rapprochement child is pulled in two opposite directions: away from mother toward autonomy and individuation and back toward her where security lies. The Don Juan pattern is a manifestation of the conflict. The individual assures himself that he can capture the desired object, often by seduction, but then he needs to get away from her. This pattern can be played out with an on-again, off-again pattern of therapy. It is a way to manage the therapist to achieve both ends: capture her and escape from her. Understanding the pattern as a manifestation of the core relationship problem is the first step toward working with this resistance.

The Achievement of Identity and Object Constancy

The *achievement of identity and object constancy* marks the end of the separation and individuation process. The cognitive development that comes with the development of language sets the stage for an integrated sense of self, or identity, and an integrated view of the other. With the final stages of differentiation of self from the primary object, certain identifications remain as part of the self. Now the capacity to comfort oneself and to relieve one's own anxiety with a variety of psychological mechanisms is part of the self, derived from what once came from outside. These identifications go hand-in-hand with the achievement of object constancy.

Mahler views object constancy in terms of the internal good object, the maternal image that is now psychically available to the child, just as the actual mother was previously available for sustenance, comfort, and love. As Tolpin (1971) puts it, object constancy constitutes a developmental leap that involves the gradual internalization of equilibrium-maintaining maternal functions, which leads to a separate, self-regulating self.

Burgner and Edgcumbe (1972) refer to "the capacity for constant relationships" and see this as a "crucial switch point in the development of object relationships." They describe this capacity functionally as "the capacity to recognize and tolerate loving and hostile feelings toward the same object; the capacity to keep feelings centered on a specific object; and the capacity to value an object for attributes other than its function of satisfying needs" (328). Anna Freud (1968) wrote, "Object constancy means . . . to retain attachment even when the person is unsatisfying."

Mahler (1968) writes of the time lag between attainment of *object permanence* in Piaget's sense and object constancy in Hartmann's sense: "Attainment of *libidinal object constancy* is much more gradual than the achievement of object permanency—and, at the beginning at least, it is a faculty that is waxing and waning and rather 'impermanent.' Up to about thirty months, it is very much at the mercy of the toddler's own mood swings and 'ego states' and dependent on the actual mother-toddler situation of the moment" (24).

Mahler points out (222) that in the earliest stages of the separation–individuation process, there is a dangerous situation of object loss, whereas the "specific danger situation toward the end of the separation–individuation phase, as object constancy is approached, is akin to the danger of *loss of the love of the libidinal object*, although there may still remain some fear of object loss as well." This is an important distinction, as the individual who has achieved object constancy carries the internalized object with him despite an interrupted relationship, and can maintain a sense of what Winnicott (1965) calls ego-relatedness.

The parent's "good for you!" that reflects pleasure in the child's accomplishments is also internalized, and now is voiced by the superego, which is composed of both the ego-ideal and the conscience. Not only does the superego criticize the self for transgressions. It also praises the self when one lives up to one's ego ideal, and is the source of a healthy and secure self-esteem.

The therapist must consider the complexities of the concept of object constancy in terms of derailment from the developmental continuum and the resulting emergence of the core relationship problem. From this viewpoint, he can conceptualize, at least for himself, the relevant character and transference resistances. Can object constancy be relied on, or will it wax and wane? If it can be relied on, the transference issue will be fear of the loss of the positive regard of the therapist. If it cannot be relied on, character resistances may come into play as a defense against the fear of object loss. To the degree that the significant attributes of the object belong to the object rather than the self, the individual will remain dependent on the significant other for the provision of these attributes and what they contribute to that person's security and self-esteem. Clinically, these patients will present with a picture of exaggerated dependency and depression in the context of a relatively well-differentiated and structured ego, although under circumstances of regression, ego functions may be compromised. These dependencies will be played out in both here-and-now interpersonal relationships and, in particular, with the therapist.

In healthy development, although archaic self- and object representations persist in the unconscious, their impact is mitigated by the ascendancy of reality-dominated perception and thought. The unconscious images may appear in dreams or in fantasy or may be re-created in artistic productions. The fairy godmother and the wicked witch of the fairy tales of childhood strike a familiar chord in children and adults alike, resonating with the now unconscious split images that dominated the earliest months of life. At times, we may yearn for the blissful oneness of an undifferentiated symbiosis, or chafe under what feels like engulfment in a relationship. But by and large, our reality perceptions keep us firmly rooted in our own individuality and that of the other. The earliest, unconscious images are no longer acted out in reality.

Despite the successful negotiation of this stage of development, there may be sources of intrapsychic conflict with such an individual, which will be the impetus to see a therapist. Resistances will be more specifically related to the specific conflict or conflicts and can more readily be worked with by interpretation or confrontation. The resistances will not spring from a need to protect a fragile character structure. A transference resistance will be more directly related to the conflict in question when the patient attributes to the therapist a particular stance with respect to the conflict. For example, this attribution might be one of disapproval, which is a projection of the individual's feelings of guilt.

The Oedipal Conflict

With the full differentiation of self from object, there is also a firmer differentiation of mother from father. The individuality of each parent is recognized and valued differentially. This is the point at which the conflict associated with the *interpersonal triangle* comes to the fore—the *Oedipus complex* (Freud 1913). What was a dyadic view of the interpersonal world now includes *two* significant others. A two-way competitiveness for the love of the other within the triangle generates new wishes, anxieties, and defenses. Along with envy, the child also experiences jealousy of a rival who is also loved; an uncomfortable ambivalence is generated. The relative ease or difficulty of this period will be strongly influenced by prior development. The Oedipal period tends to overlap with the latter part of the rapprochement phase. Rapprochement anxieties are aggravated by the interpersonal conflicts of the triangle. The child's ability to negotiate this troublesome period will also be affected by parental attitudes toward the child, who now presents the parents with an increasingly complex little person. It will also be affected by the parents' unresolved triangle dynamics when they cannot tolerate the child's wishes and moves toward the other parent. The child feels forced to choose one parent over the other, but with choosing comes losing. It is a painful and insoluble dilemma for the child, creating the anxieties that will later bring him or her into treatment.

The therapist may find himself in a triangle created by the patient that puts him in the middle between her and another patient or between her and his family. He will be able to use the dynamic she sets up, perhaps to triumph in the competition, as a window into the dynamic she played out with her parents. The resistance aspect can be interpreted as well as the connection between the past and the present.

The child will also be taken up into the dynamics of the family system as a whole. The understanding of the transference and transference resistances relies on the uncovering of the wider interpersonal system and subsystems of the family and the patient's place within this wider context. Perhaps he was assigned a particular role in the family. He was probably derailed as he moved toward individuation and came to feel defined by this "irrational role" (Framo 1970). Generally, these irrational role assignments do not come into play until the child has reached the age where language begins to play a role and the evolving uniqueness of the child is more salient. The child's innate talents, constitutional factors, and temperament will lend themselves to service parental wishes and fears. For example, if a mother who has only sons selects one of them to take the role of the wished-for daughter, she is not likely to choose the robust, action-oriented son, but the quieter one who is content to read or color. In the 1960s, family therapists became aware of the role of the "identified patient" who was said to be the cause of the family's unhappiness. Roles such as the "smart one" or the "clumsy one," the "good one" or the "bad one," would lead to an acting out of the assigned role and, with it, a derailment of the child's authentic self.

As his core relationship problem, the patient will play out his assigned role in the therapy relationship as well. It will be incumbent on the therapist to widen his or her understanding of the patient's life to take in the complexities of psychological development that take place in later childhood and into adolescence as well.

As soon as possible, the therapist must begin to construct a hypothesis as to the patient's core relationship problem. We do not want to overestimate the pathology or the strength, nor do we want to underestimate them. The more on target we are, the less likely are we to make a therapeutic error that has the potential for stopping the treatment before it has even begun. The next chapter describes a number of approaches to making the hypothesis.

2

Constructing the
Developmental Hypothesis

Once we have alerted ourselves to the importance of identifying the core relationship problem, identifying where along the developmental continuum the individual became derailed and the relationship problem that resulted from the derailment, we may wonder how we can get the data that will help us come to this understanding. We will have to identify the adaptations the child made in the service of his survival and the maintenance of his connection with the needed other. We will have to identify the defenses he erected against anxiety and depression as well.

The developmental continuum in terms of attachment, separation, and individuation (and childhood and adolescence described in the last chapter), lays out the stages of the formative years of life. It is these stages we must refer to when we seek to discover the point of emotional and relational derailment. What is set up within the interpersonal matrix of the primary relationship becomes structured within the psyche. The self and the object representations thus structured, and their connecting affect, thoughts, and desires, then become manifest interpersonally later in life. What is observed in here-and-now relationships is a key to the nature of the adult's internal world. We shift our emphasis from what is structural, in object-relational terms, to what is dynamically relational.

THE HISTORY

A detailed history will give us not only information, but also the start of making our hypothesis about the core problem. As we get new information along the way, we may want to amend the hypothesis. For example, if the individual tells us he is the fourth child of seven, that they were all eighteen months apart, and that the mother was the only caregiver, we can certainly use this information to start to build the story of this person's psychological development. The mother was probably overwhelmed and unavailable. In addition, the chaos and even assaultiveness of the sibling milieu would very likely lead to trauma and subsequent character defenses against that traumatic state. There may be a situation of chronic breakdown when defensive detachment fails. We can at least hypothesize that development in the most critical years was at best seriously deficient if not disastrously compromised. Of course, we will also want to look for and understand the individual's strengths, compensatory and/or defensive structures, mechanisms, or strategies that enable the person to function at a higher level than the far less optimal beginning might suggest. The child caught in a chaotic milieu may learn to detach and go into his or her own mind: that is, develop a schizoid defense against the inner turmoil. If the child is endowed with good intelligence, he may live his life through the intellect alone. He may learn about realities different from that of his family through books. He may even be a high achiever in his profession. However, thrust into a relational situation, the structural pathology is likely to reveal itself.

If, in these cases, a therapist is fooled by what appears at first to be a high level of development and healthy character structure, his error will be exposed in short order by the eruption of an unexpected and difficult transference reaction or evidence of a character resistance.

Any significant departure from what we may view as an average expectable sequence of life events needs attention and exploration. Illness and traumatic separations such as hospitalization may pinpoint a traumatic derailment. Removing a child from what has been a stable foster home situation for years, as has been done when a biological parent shows up and claims the child, will shatter the child's sense of who he is. His whole reality changes. He may be said to have made a satisfactory adjustment, but the superficial adaptations of necessity will conceal the split in his very character structure. As an adult, this individual's way of getting along in the world will likely be to make similar adaptations to the other. Of course, this will play out as a transference resistance should he find his way to a therapist. However the material will be approached, an empathic attitude toward the child, his fears, and his survival mechanisms is essential. The earlier the disruption of the child's life, the more likely the derailment came at an earlier point on the developmental continuum. There may be a character resistance that defends against a dissolution of the self.

A six-year-old boy was referred for therapy because of fearfulness. He reported a recurring, terrifying nightmare of giant hands coming to get him. One might jump to conclusions about a persecutory primary relationship. However, he was a premature baby, weighing just less than two pounds at birth. He spent many months in an incubator before he was big and strong enough to be taken out of it. If we picture that incubator, we can see the two holes in its side that allow the one who was taking care of this tiny infant to put her hands through to feed him, clean him, or in general give him the care he needed to survive. Able to fit in an adult's two hands, his visual image of what was, in effect, his primary object would be that of two giant hands. The image remained as what Grotstein (1981) refers to as a background object of primal identification to come forth in consciousness and frighten him. That he had an unusually acute memory was demonstrated by his remembering the questions he had been asked when given the Stanford Binet Intelligence Test a year previously. The importance of a detailed history as accurate as possible is demonstrated by this case.

Ted Kaczynski's mother wrote about the transformation of her nine-month-old baby son Ted as the result of his weeklong hospitalization. She said he was a happy baby when she took him to the hospital, but when she brought him home he was limp and unresponsive, "like a bundle of clothes." She was allowed to visit him only once in that week. He would not look at her when she arrived and days later when she returned to take him home.

A few years later, the family pediatrician showed her and Ted, who was then four, the photograph the hospital had left in his record. Ted was pinned down so the physicians could photograph his hives. "Ted glanced at it and looked away," she recalled. "He refused to look at it any more, and I thought, 'Oh my God, he's having the same feelings that he had when he was held down that way.'"

When Ted was about 10, his father caught a shrew in their back yard. He popped a sieve over it and called out to the children nearby to come and see it. When he saw the trapped shrew Ted screamed, "Let it go! Let it go!" His father handed it to him to let it run free. His mother had seen this kind of reaction before. She wondered if he was again having the same feelings he did when he stood up in his crib at the hospital and was crying and reaching out his arms as the nurse pushed her out the door.

Ted became ill after his freshman year of college and his mother wanted to take him to the doctor. She said, "Ted shut down, refusing to talk to anyone. It was as though a kind of veil or film would come down across his face." His brother added, "There was a sense that he was profoundly closed off." It was one of many withdrawals that would recur throughout his life, sometimes for no discernible reason. He would stare silently at the ground, apparently lost in his own world. His mother and brother both commented on his almost paralyzing uneasiness around strangers, a reaction his mother traces back to his childhood hospitalization when she was not allowed to stay with him through days of medical observation and treatment.

The family came to see him as a person of "strange contradictions" who could be moody and unhappy and then inexplicably pleasant and compassionate. His brother said, "I think of Ted as a young boy crying over a rabbit or the expression of concern he had about our cousin when she was injured and how I knew he was certainly a person who was capable of a conscience, who was capable of human sympathy. But you had a sense that these capabilities were not integrated into a whole personality."

Bowlby (1973) noted a predictable sequence of reactions to separation in children between the ages of six months and three to four years. Children who had not yet consolidated the attachment bond prior to the age of six months did not show these typical reactions. The children observed had been placed in an institutional setting because of a family emergency of one kind or another. This sequence of reaction was first *protest*, secondly *despair*, and finally, *detachment*. The protesting child screams, cries, and cannot be comforted. He may resist caretaking efforts for as long as two weeks. The despairing child is preoccupied with his mother and is vigilant for her return. He will alternately cling to and then fling away his teddy bear or security blanket. And although he may permit himself to be tended to by one preferred caretaker, his feelings toward this person clearly will be mixed.

The final stage, detachment, becomes evident as the child settles down and seems to be adjusting reasonably well. However, when his mother returns at this point, he behaves as though he does not recognize her or he retreats tearfully from her. He may still respond with affection to the father, however. After the reunion and following the period of detachment, there is usually a phase of marked ambivalence toward the mother, who may find it difficult to deal with his difficult behavior.

Rutter (1973) points out that severe distress of the child can be mitigated through the intense interaction between the child and *one* person throughout the separation experience. It is not likely that Ted was fortunate enough to have that compensatory relationship available to him. To assess the developmental consequences of the trauma, we ask with respect to early childhood trauma who the child was to whom it happened. In Ted's case, he was a nine-month-old baby. He was taken from everyone he knew at the peak of a baby's separation and stranger anxieties and was subjected to frightening and painful procedures. One can well surmise that the split that took place in his budding sense of self and other resulted in evidence of a good and loving start, cut short by what must have been a living hell for this terrified baby. It is not unreasonable to hypothesize that this derailment and its consequences are what led to the birth and evolution of the Unabomber.

A history of separation in early childhood, whatever the causes, should alert the therapist to the possibility of derailment from the developmental continuum at that phase of life, with its resulting core relationship problem and the potential for character or transference resistances stemming from that problem. Looking for the kinds of defenses and adaptations the child devised to maintain both intrapsychic and interpersonal safety should be part of that exploration. Using the core relationship problem as an organizing principle, one should be able to make sense of later elaborations and manifestations of the problem.

THE FAMILY STRUCTURE

Birth order and the role of siblings is given short shrift in psychoanalytic theory. I have found many times that the birth of a second child is far more traumatic for the firstborn than is often recognized. We are familiar with the concept of sibling rivalry. Even more important is the degree to which the birth of the new baby may constitute a severe narcissistic wound for the firstborn. Heretofore, he experienced the specialness attendant on being, at least for a time, the only child. Sometimes, paradoxically, the better the relationship with the mother in the first years, the greater the felt betrayal and the greater the wound. A story from the previous chapter is related—the history of the man who came to the conclusion that he was "not enough." However, the splitting off and repression of the hurt and angry three-year-old will not have the same implications for treatment as a more primitive splitting, or more precisely, a failure of integration. Despite unresolved dependency issues vis-à-vis the mother who disappointed, the analytic work in these cases can usually rely on an observing ego, a cohesive self, a reliable therapeutic alliance, and, despite significant transference resistance, an absence of primitive enactments. This is a good example of how important it is to ascertain the point on the developmental continuum where psychological derailment occurred.

We may hear information that alerts us to significant core pathology when the patient's family was chaotic, with several poorly cared-for children, an alcoholic mother, or battling parents. We can expect the external chaos to be mirrored in the internal chaos of the patient's personality. We will look for the kinds of defenses and adaptations that enabled the person to survive the family milieu, but we should not underestimate the core weakness, even in the face of apparently successful later adaptation. Were there other caretakers, perhaps a loving grandmother or teachers who encouraged them once they went to school? Despite these sources of emotional strength, the underlying vulnerability remains to emerge under trying circumstances. Are there character resistances that protect the individual from the emergence of the chaos? Do they exist side-by-side with transference resistances? Learning how to please teachers may have created an interpersonal safe harbor. Having to please the therapist later on will emerge as a transference resistance. Dealing with the feared dangers to the internal structure will have to be attended to most carefully. A premature confrontation of transference resistances may traumatize the patient.

The severity of a loss of a parent, whether by death or divorce, will depend on where the child was developmentally. As a point of derailment, it will be important to note what developmental tasks were foreclosed as the result of this loss. For example, the loss of the father will throw the child back more dependently on the mother, complicating the processes of separation and individuation.

SETTING THE STRUCTURE OF THERAPY

How the therapy structure is set up with respect to frequency of meetings and fee payment will be rich in clinically relevant information. If the patient wants to come in only once a week but submits to the therapist's insistence that it must be more in order for the work to be productive, the therapist may find that she has activated a core conflict characterized by a pattern of overt compliance and covert defiance that simultaneously connects and distances the person from the other. There is a wish *and* a fear with respect to intimate relationships. While the establishment of a safe frame for the work is critical, one can confuse this with acting out one's own agenda, which may be more of what is at issue. Transference and countertransference resistances may be manifest in the very first session. Economic considerations may play a role. The source of the referral can also bear on the therapist's approach to the treatment at the outset.

Stating the Hypothesis

It is not the historical event per se that is so critical. We have to ask, who was the child at the time of the event? Taking the history is not done by formula. The therapist follows the lines of exploration even as the history-taking is underway. He pays attention to the words the patient uses, to what they signify to the patient as well as what they indicate to the therapist. Therapy starts the moment the person arrives for the first session. Indeed, it starts with the referral and making the appointment. But it is in the first contact that the sensitive and alert therapist will start making, at least mentally, notes of the process as it unfolds. Questions can be formulated to evoke relationship data and to see if patterns readily emerge, which they often do. Specific questions about the way the individual related to mother, to father, and to little brother and how other family members related to one another may reveal important information about the family system and the person's place in it. It is a matter of how one listens and synthesizes that may render the intake dry and unproductive or rich in clues about the core relationship conflict, how it arose, and what its psychological consequences have been throughout life. A willingness to wander about in the interviews, to clarify and inquire when it makes sense, can make even a somewhat formal interview rich in what is gleaned from it. Often, by the end of the first session, the therapist can make a simple statement such as, "What I see as a thread that runs through all you have been telling me is that you have difficulty holding on to your sense of yourself when you are with people important to you." It does not go too deep. It does not uncover. It puts into a unifying statement all that the person has been telling you in many different ways. In my experience, patients react to this by feeling understood and hopeful that the therapist can help them. The core relationship problem has been put on the table, to be used as an organizing principle as the work goes along.

Remember, developmental derailment can occur anywhere along the developmental continuum. Under the heading "core relationship problem," we will find issues of very early developmental failure and deficit, or issues of somewhat later emerging conflicts. Self psychologists pay special attention to deficits of the self. A core relationship conflict may evolve as the child strives for autonomy. Relationship, however, is still the operative word. The earlier the core relationship problem develops, the more problematic the organization of the self, whether it be a chaotic disorganization under stress or a paranoid organization that resulted because the infant's world consisted of interactions with a frightening, hurtful caretaker or environment. Because this latter unfortunate situation usually alternates with times of aloneness and abandonment, we are also likely to see an underlying anaclitic depression. Defenses against both of these dangers, such as schizoid detachment, as well as compensatory mechanisms, such as over-reliance on the intellect, will be evident in the individual's way of being in the world. Later on we may find this person clinging to internal or external persecutory relationships in preference to experiencing what Grotstein calls the "black hole," the empty despair of the anaclitic depression. Any object is better than no object.

Kohut (1977) calls our attention to the distinction between "primary structure" that arises out of the earliest relationship with the mother, and later, defensive, secondary, or compensatory structures that may arise out of other important relationships, especially with the father—as well as those with a grandparent, teachers, or mentors—or as a way to defend against the distress of the primary relational set-up. It will be important to know what these are, to understand the complexities of that individual's way of being in the world, to know where there is vulnerability and to know where there is strength.

Bromberg (1983) speaks of the importance of knowing where the patient is on the "empathy-anxiety gradient" at any given moment in the treatment situation. He refers to Sullivan's (1954) observations that the analyst must be responsive to where the patient is on a gradient of anxiety, trying to maintain it at an optimally minimal level: low enough so that the patient's defenses do not foreclose analytic inquiry, but high enough so that the defensive structure itself can be identified and explored. Bromberg writes of the maintenance of the optimal balance between empathy and anxiety as an approach to treatment that is independent of the analyst's personal metapsychology.

We have to know when to function as a selfobject (in Kohutian terms) and when it is safe to interpret conflict. The same patient may shift from session to session or even within a single session, and therapeutic errors occur when we are wrong about that determination. When an individual is in a higher-level state, he may feel insulted by an empathic response. If he is in a vulnerable state, he may be traumatized by an interpretation. The transference implications must be explored right away. If he is insulted by the therapist's empathy, the therapist might wonder aloud, "I'm puzzled what troubled you about what I just said." If the patient is traumatized by an interpretation, one cannot be as direct. Depending on the specifics of the situation and the patient's core issues, one might say something like, "I'm sorry if I upset you," acknowledging the failure of empathy when empathy was indicated. Then the patient may again feel safe enough to volunteer what was so upsetting about the therapist's comment.

CONSTITUTIONAL FACTORS

We tend to overlook the constitutional, temperamental givens of the child as contributor to the early relationship milieu. One can observe the very young child from the perspective of Karen Horney's *types* (1945). These behavioral styles are especially obvious when the child is upset. There is the child who resorts to anxious clinging (who moves *toward people*), the one who retreats to a distance with the thumb in the mouth (who moves *away from people*), and the one who may physically attack the mother (who moves *against people*). That these styles affect the mother is certain, not only because they evoke emotions, but also because of how they may be negatively labeled—as "demanding," "rejecting," or "bad." When the mother–child relationship gets off to a bad start because of the behavioral style the child was born with, development all along the continuum may be, to some degree, less that optimal. Where the lack of good fit between them leads to eventual derailment will bear some relation to the strength or vulnerabilities with which the child negotiates that turn of events.

These styles may be manifest in the treatment situation, either evoking in the therapist responses similar to those of the mother (which would be problematic), or enabling in the intuitive and empathic therapist a useful attitude and posture. In our eagerness to understand the individual in terms of early interpersonal experience, we should not forget about these innate givens that were, and probably still are, part of the mix. They will color the transference resistances and the countertransference resistances.

ASSESSMENT OF STRENGTHS AND WEAKNESSES

Understanding where the child was developmentally when the conflict arose also tells us what strengths and vulnerabilities existed at the time of derailment. Was he a toddler with limited language abilities, or was he just starting school? What were her abilities to reason and to process her own experience? Was he still prone to magical thinking? Did she think concretely or could she understand cause and effect? This is where background knowledge about overall child development is crucial for a therapist. When a patient describes traumatic events that occurred during childhood, we need to ask, "Who was the child to whom this happened? Was he or she a relatively healthy child, both physically and emotionally? Or was the child already seriously compromised because of preexisting psychological disorder?" A psychologically robust child can weather distressing events that a fragile child cannot. Where was the child in terms of cognitive development? Social development? Motor development? Language development? If we can answer these questions, we will have a clearer picture not only of pathology and vulnerability, but also of health and strength in terms of resources that were the outcome of successful negotiation of earlier development.

EGO AND SUPEREGO FUNCTIONS OPERATIONALLY DEFINED

Serious errors can be avoided if the therapist knows where he has to be unusually careful in his interventions, or whether he can risk upsetting the patient in the service of the treatment. An accurate assessment of ego functions after the initial intake, or as soon as possible thereafter, will lessen the possibility of such errors. The following outline (Horner 1985) can be useful in making these determinations.

EGO FUNCTIONS

Relation to reality

1. Good reality testing
   Patient can distinguish between wishes, fears, and reality.
2. Sense of self as real
   Allowing for defensive depersonalization, patient experiences himself as real most of the time.
3. Can look at self objectively
   Patient can stand back and ally himself with the interviewer to explore the patient's wishes, feelings, beliefs, and actions.

Regulation and control of instinctual drives

1. Capacity for delay
   Patient adapts readily to the delays of the intake process and can tolerate frustration of wishes.
2. Adequate impulse control
   Patient can talk about sexual or aggressive impulses without having to discharge them into action.
3. Capacity for adaptive expression
   Control of sexual and aggressive impulses is not too rigid to allow for their appropriate expression in reality.

Object relations

1. Basic trust
   Patient sees at least one person as benign and trustworthy.
2. Relatedness
   Patient is emotionally present and interpersonally engaged during the interview.
3. Differentiation
   Patient is able to perceive the interviewer and others as separate and different from himself.
4. Stability
   Patient can work with transference interpretations without losing a realistic perception of the interviewer.
5. Integration
   Patient can tolerate ambivalence toward himself and others.
6. Maturity
   Patient has been able to establish and maintain true peer relationships. Patient has a history of altruistic relationships.

Thought processes

1. Patient can think conceptually and logically.

Defenses

1. Adequacy
   Patient can tolerate negative and positive affect (anxiety, depression, guilt, shame, anger, love, affection, pleasure).
   Patient can talk about negative and positive affects.
   Patient can recover readily from a regressive reaction and talk about it.
2. Flexibility
   Flexibility of defenses allows for their examination in the interview.
3. Maturity
   Major defenses used are the more advanced ones of intellectualization, sublimation, repression, rationalization, or displacement without significant recourse to more primitive modes of projection, externalization, somatization, denial, splitting, or introjection.

Autonomous Functions

1. Relative independence from conflict
   Speech, cognition, perception, or motor behavior are not impaired in life or in the interview because of psychological reasons.
2. Recoverability
   If these functions are partially impaired, this can be understood and worked with in a psychological context by the patient.
3. Organic integrity
   There are no neurological disorders that would cause impairment that interfered with the ability to do the work of the interview.

Synthetic Functions

1. Psychological mindedness
   Patient is able to think in terms of psychological cause and effect.
2. Capacity for insight
   Patient is able to draw valid psychological conclusions with respect to his own feelings, wishes, thoughts, and behavior.

SUPEREGO FUNCTIONS

Conscience

1. Standards of right and wrong
   Patient wants to live according to established standards of right and wrong.
2. Capacity for guilt
   Patient experiences guilt when he fails to meet these standards.
3. Realistic
   Standards do not require unrealistic moral perfection.

Ego-Ideal

1. Feelings of worth
   Patient has well-established sense of himself as a worthwhile person.
2. Realistic
   Patient's image of himself does not require unrealistic perfection or reveal grandiosity.

Working over many years with practicing psychotherapists in my consultation groups, I found that their difficulties were due as much if not more to their countertransference resistances than to ignorance. Before addressing specific examples of transference resistance, in the next chapter I delineate some of these barriers to professional competence.

3

Countertransference Resistance and Therapeutic Impasse

In *The Future Prospects of Psycho-Analytic Therapy,* Freud ([1910] 1957) wrote: "We have become aware of the 'counter-transference,' which arises in him as a result of the patient's influence on his unconscious feelings, and we are almost inclined to insist that he shall recognize this counter-transference in himself and overcome it. . . . [We] have noticed that no psycho-analyst goes further than his own complexes and *internal resistances* permit" (144) (italics added).

In my twenty years of conducting consultation groups with practicing psychotherapists, I came to realize that the problems they were presenting to me were often as much due to their unique resistances to doing the analytic work as to their ignorance of theory. While many of their patients did indeed present with very difficult behaviors and material, impasses—often lasting years—were largely due to the therapists' countertransference issues. And more often than not, these issues were rooted in the therapists' core relationship problem as it became acted out in their work.

The therapist's way of being in the world vis-à-vis others may be built into her character or activated only in response to certain kinds of stress in the relationship. In the first instance, clinical work as a whole will be compromised. In the second, only work with certain patients will be affected. In either case, it behooves us as clinicians to be able to identify and understand our own core relationship problems and monitor their activation in the clinical situation (Horner 1998).

COUNTERTRANSFERENCE RESISTANCE

Transference resistance has been defined as the patient's way of relating to the therapist so as to bring about a wished-for interaction or to prevent one that is feared. It is a way to manage the therapist and the process. Countertransference resistance often has the same aim in its attempt to manage the interaction—to prevent an unwanted interaction or to bring about one that would be pleasant or gratifying. At an unconscious level, the therapist may relate to the patient *as if* the patient were the therapist's authority figure. In this case, she brings to the interaction archaic adaptations and defenses that were set up in childhood vis-à-vis her own mother or father. The resulting enactments arise out of an unconscious collusion between patient and therapist. With this development, the treatment process is stalemated.

Fear of the Object's Narcissistic Rage

Fear of the object's narcissistic rage becomes fear of the patient's narcissistic rage. As a child, the now-therapist learned to cater to the mother's demands, to behave so as not to upset her and provoke her hateful wrath. She now projects onto the patient—rightfully or wrongly—the same demands and expects the same reactions. In effect, the therapist once again becomes the frightened child and caters to the unrealistic demands of the difficult patient. She will theoretically justify her submission as her attempt to be empathic, when limit-setting, interpretation, or confrontation may be indicated. She feels as powerless as she did as a child. And, indeed, she becomes impotent as a therapist.

Need to Justify Oneself to the Other

A *need to justify oneself* is also brought forward from experiences with a critical parent. In many instances in the clinical situation, the therapist is faced with the patient's questioning or criticism of therapy. Instead of exploring what is going on with the patient, the therapist may give "logical" explanations about how therapy works. She may feel she has to justify her fee. Issues of setting or maintaining the frame often fall into this category. She does not explore what was so distressful for the patient about this limit. Instead, she gives a lengthy explanation about the reason for the rules of the frame in order to justify her position.

One man asked many personal questions, such as where the therapist lived. He wanted to be able to drive by and see her house. When this was explored, it turned out he feared that, deep down, the therapist really was someone who would hurt him. He was gathering information so as to find a way to be able to feel safe. His mother's irrational outbursts frightened him as a child. He assumed that the same thing would happen with his therapist. One would never know from his friendly demeanor that such a negative transference was operating. He insisted he was just being "curious." He believed that "knowing *about*" the therapist was the same as knowing her, and thus knowing what to expect from her.

Pressure to Perform

The therapist may, out of her own core relationship problem, feel a *pressure to perform*.

As a child, she felt she had to prove her value to her mother or her father, perhaps by excelling at sports or her studies. Now she feels she has to prove her worth to the patient. She tries to make brilliant interpretations. Too often these interpretations miss the patient. Winnicott (1971) writes that "it is only in being creative that the individual discovers the self." He adds that "a patient's creativity can be stolen by a therapist who knows too much" (57). To therapists who worry about having "the right answer," I will say, "The answer is always in the patient. All you need to know is the right question to ask."

The critical patient who questions the value of therapy or the therapist's competence may once again stir up this pressure to perform. When this happens, the therapist may worry more about the astuteness of her interventions than their appropriateness or helpfulness.

The source of the referral may also be the source of a pressure to perform. The therapist wants to look good to her colleague, not only to make sure there will be future referrals, but also out of a concern about the colleague's judgment of her competence.

Resistance to Setting the Frame

The therapist may balk at setting an appropriate frame if it makes her feel too much like the rigid and controlling father she resented so deeply. She will worry about the hostile resentment of the patient, projecting her own childhood resentments toward her authority figures. An overly permissive reaction formation on her part may lead the patient to believe that his transference fantasies and wishes have become realized. In some cases this may lead to a psychotic transference in which the reality of the relationship is either lost or can be denied. The therapist may justify the looseness of the frame with theoretical jargon about the value of providing a corrective emotional experience for the patient.

Self-Effacement

The self-effacing therapist who grew up believing that her thoughts, feelings, and wishes did not matter was derailed from the developmental continuum as she began to emerge as a little person in her own right. She may now find it difficult to accept how important she is to her patients. She may be oblivious to transference dreams. She will certainly have difficulty with an idealizing transference and may actively try to explain it away. She will deny the idealized qualities attributed to her by the patient, which make it possible for him to allow himself to depend on her. She may feel guilty about asking for money, allowing large balances to build up. Sooner or later, she will come to feel taken advantage of by her patients.

Having to Be "Good"

The therapist who must maintain a self-image as "good" or as morally superior is likely to be blocked from the use of a clinically appropriate aggression that is manifest in confrontation. This is the kind of access to a healthy aggression that is needed by the surgeon as he takes up his scalpel. It is not imbued with hostility or a wish to hurt. She is blocked in general from a healthy self-protective or self-expressive aggression. No matter how careful and gentle a confrontation, it is inherently aggressive inasmuch as it is used against the patient's defensive strategies. This therapist is more comfortable when she is "supportive," "validating," or "confirming." She will even find a theoretical rationalization for her countertransference resistance to being otherwise. While she may try to avert the patient's aggression by stifling her own, validation of the patient's infantile, narcissistic rage may reinforce it, validating the infantile claims and expectations as well.

Need to Be Acknowledged

Giovacchini (1972) described the *existential annihilation* sometimes experienced by the therapist who is working with a patient who denies the separate existence of the therapist. Derailed from the developmental continuum early in the separation–individuation process, the patient is threatened by conscious awareness of the therapist's separateness. He may hold on to a fantasy that the therapist is essentially an extension of himself. In self-psychology terms, the therapist lends herself to function as a selfobject for the patient as long as it is necessary. A transference interpretation is experienced as an assault or an abandonment. To the patient, it says, "You must pay attention to *me!*"

The therapist who cannot tolerate this necessary annihilation may feel impelled to insist her presence be noted in one way or another. It may be through a contraindicated transference interpretation. It may be in some form of self-disclosure that is unconsciously motivated to remove the intense discomfort of the imposed nonexistence. The therapist's own need to have her existence acknowledged will interfere with her ability to stay with the patient. This therapist may do fine with another kind of patient, but because of her own vulnerability in this regard, will find it intolerable to work with this individual.

The Wish to Be Idealized and Failure to Maintain Neutrality

While the therapist's need to be acknowledged may be in reaction to felt discomfort, perhaps anxiety, the wish to be idealized comes from his or her own wish for narcissistic pleasure. Greenberg (1986) believes that neutrality is "a way of affirming our own commitment to [the patient's] exploration and self knowledge in contrast to other therapeutic aims" (82). He agrees with Schafer (1983) that there is an intimate connection between the analyst's neutrality and the patient's experience of safety, without which he or she would continue to "feel injured, betrayed, threatened, seduced, or otherwise interfered with or traumatized" (32). If the therapist understands the patient's core relationship problem and the resulting vulnerabilities, he is less likely to make a departure from neutrality that will threaten the patient in the manner described by Schafer.

Some therapists believe that it is important to give the patient the experience of a helpful "real" relationship. Greenson (1967) describes two aspects of what is real in the real relationship. It may mean "realistic, reality oriented or undistorted as contrasted to the term 'transference' which connotes unrealistic, distorted, and inappropriate. The word may also refer to genuine, authentic, and true in contrast to artificial, synthetic or assumed" (169). The transference relationship may feel genuine, but it will not be realistic. On the other hand, the working alliance is realistic but it may not feel genuine. Greenson uses the term "real relationship" in reference to that aspect that is both genuine *and* real.

But where is the line between what Held-Weiss (1986) calls spontaneity in the analyst and the analyst's acting out of his own needs and desires? The therapist who values realness between himself and his patient is under greater pressure to monitor the potential danger. When the therapist's countertransference is perceived in his departure from neutrality and is commented on by the patient, acknowledgment of the interpersonal process prevents attribution of the patient's reaction entirely to what is contained within her psyche, the kind of interpretation that may be experienced by the patient as "crazy-making."

When the therapist's professional ego-ideal is complicated by his wish to be not only appreciated, but idealized, by virtue of his attempts to *be* that ideal he has lost who and where the patient is. And when that ideal is either to be a better mother than the patient had, or a better father than the patient had—thus acting out what he believes the patient's idealized object to be—the countertransference resistance is his way of managing the relationship by so doing. It will, in his fantasy, bring about a mutually idealizing relationship. This is not unlike what happens with "love at first sight." Each of the pair sees his or her idealized self reflected in the gaze of the other, who then becomes the idealized selfobject.

The therapist may rationalize that he has meant to "mirror" back the strengths and virtues of the patient as a way to encourage her to "realize her potential." But does he realize that this so-called mirroring of her intellectual potential is experienced by the patient as a pressure to perform to make him feel good? Does he realize that this so-called mirroring of how beautiful and sexy she is does not enhance her self-esteem as a woman as he likes to believe, but repeats the trauma of being sexualized by an inappropriate father? He does not understand that her acting-out is a reenactment of how she dealt with the fear she felt vis-à-vis her father. He denies that his behavior is the cause of her not feeling safe as Schafer says the patient should, but causes her to feel seduced.

In contrast to the therapist's acting out his own needs or desires in the above ways, Poland (1984) defines true neutrality as originating "in genuine respect for the patient's individuality . . . [a] fundamental regard for the essential otherness of the patient, for the uniqueness of the patient's self in its own right" (285–86). These conditions are essential to prevent the therapeutic impasse that comes from the therapist's countertransference resistance.

Authority Figures

A therapist adapted to her domineering and critical mother by passively submitting to her will. She attributed the same demand to her patient and again she adopted a posture of submission. The patient was acting out in therapy, running roughshod over her. When this was brought up in supervision, she reacted to the supervisor as a frightened child, feeling she had to submit once again. She could not learn, as learning was submission. She found herself in a difficult dilemma. She had to submit to her supervisor about not submitting to the patient. Her core relationship problem resulted in a countertransference resistance as well as a resistance to learning.

A therapist's relationship to her supervisor can also be a source of clinical difficulties. Whether the therapist takes a stance of obedient compliance or oppositional defiance, the patient will pay the price. The therapist may apply something the supervisor has said in a manner that ensures its failure. There is a secret pleasure in proving the supervisor wrong and in protesting, "But I did what you told me to do."

When the therapist wonders what the supervisor would do or say at a difficult moment in the treatment situation, he or she will have renounced his or her own capacity to think. The emotional and cognitive autonomy required to do optimal work can be compromised as a consequence of core relationship problems that arose at various stages along the developmental continuum. Leftover conflicts from the rapprochement phase can lead to anxiety over taking autonomous action. Unresolved Oedipal strivings can lead to a competitive need to triumph over authority figures in general. An idealization of authority figures in general can have the same stultifying effect as can an idealization of special teachers and their pet theories.

When a therapist has any of these core relationship problems, therapy becomes a three-person situation where the presence of the invisible supervisor comes between therapist and patient. To know ourselves, to monitor the activation of our own core relationship problems so as to not act them out, is our responsibility as therapists. Ultimately, our role is to help the patient come to the same level of self-awareness in the hope that he or she will be able to move beyond the impasse attendant on his or her own unresolved core relationship problem.

The following chapter addresses one of the most difficult resistances to be dealt with in psychotherapy. It is the patient's need to cling to an image of himself or herself as good—as morally superior. With it comes the denial of the dark side. Anger is expressed as righteous indignation. Fantasies of aggression, even killing, are always in the service of some noble cause.

4

Transference Resistances of the "Good Boy" and the "Good Girl"

THE HUMAN CONDITION

The fight between good and evil, love and hate, is a central theme of the developing psyche of every child and of the larger society as well. Its universality suggests something in human development itself that sets this conflict up from the start of life. The baby coos as he nuzzles the warm, soft breast of his mother. He also screams with rage when she is slow to respond to his urgently felt need. *Love and hate are there from the start in their most primitive form.*

The theme is echoed in art and literature. The eternal struggle between light and dark, good and evil, is presented in the movie *Star Wars* as an allegory. We cheer for Obi-Wan Kenobi as he battles the evil Darth Vader to the death. Tales of the triumph of good over evil, of the weak over the strong, are stories that endure and inspire. Little David defeats the giant Goliath with his slingshot. Hansel and Gretel outsmart the witch and push her into the oven, a fate she had in store for them. In *Harry Potter and the Sorcerer's Stone* (Rowling 1998), Harry battles Voldemort, the personification of the dark side, for his very life. Harry is protected by the power of his mother's love. In Angus Wilson's (1974) analysis of Charles Dickens' novel, *The Mystery of Edwin Drood*, Wilson concludes that the book is not a "whodunit," but depicts the fight between the forces of good and evil as revealed in the society of Dickens' time. Wilson places particular emphasis on the analysis and personification of evil, a preoccupation in all of Dickens' novels. And on almost daily television, a proliferation of episodes of *Law and*

Order and its spin-offs portray the battle between the forces of good and evil in today's society.

As a battle intrinsic to the human condition, this war is fought on many fronts, not the least of which takes place in the heart and mind of the individual. Arthur Miller writes: "It is always and forever the struggle to perceive somehow our own complicity with evil is a horror not to be borne. . . . [It is] much more reassuring to see the world in terms of totally innocent victims and totally evil instigators" (May 1972).

Rollo May writes of "pseudo-innocence." When we face questions too difficult to confront, we may shrink into this kind of innocence and make a virtue of powerlessness, weakness, and helplessness. Most important, May points out that it is pseudo-innocence that cannot come to terms with the destructiveness in oneself or in others. In his view, when innocence cannot include what he refers to as the demonic, it becomes evil. He also makes the salient point that the pseudo-innocent is not necessarily a moral person because there is no moral choice to be made. Former president Jimmy Carter confessed that he was guilty of "lusting in his heart"; yet, he made the moral choice to be faithful to his wife. A public posture of goodness and concern for the downtrodden does not necessarily indicate true morality.

Owning up to the dark side does not mean giving it license to act. In fact, this step helps prevent the not-uncommon periodic out-of-control escape of hostile acts or words from the depths where they are buried. This hostility is often vented on those clearly weaker than the self. The oh-so-good wife takes out her rage on her child. The horrific act of the mother who drowned her five helpless children in the bathtub was attributed to a postpartum depression. Only the existence of a dark side hidden beneath her self-sacrificing wife and mother persona would explain the will and strength it took for her to do the unthinkable. Owning the dark side makes it possible to make truly moral choices and gain the healthy aggression and energy that is needed to pursue goals that have been thwarted thus far.

In therapy, the "good girl" or the "good boy" make a virtue of powerlessness, weakness, and helplessness, exemplifying what May has defined as "pseudo-innocence." This stance can best be understood in developmental and relational terms. As a transference resistance, it is a difficult knot to untie. This is the patient who reports a dream that someone was attacking the therapist, but he came to the therapist's rescue and saved her from certain death. His dark side is externalized and slain. His good side is triumphant. Not only is the therapist protected from the destructiveness of his dark side, he also will have earned her love by virtue of his goodness and bravery. His reward will be a special place in her heart. When the reward for goodness is not forthcoming, what is revealed is that the individual feels *entitled* to the reward. It is in this sense of entitlement that the closeness of the masochistic personality to the narcissist is seen. The goodness of the self is maintained. The self is now the righteous victim of the other who has failed to live up to expectations. This complex transference resistance may not always be as blatantly obvious as revealed by the dream, but it will come out again and again in subtle or not-so-subtle ways.

The patient will carefully hide negative feelings or thoughts about the therapist. They are not split off or repressed. They are consciously hidden. The good girl tries to be a good patient as well. One woman was quite direct about her wish to please. She perceived her therapist as angry during the previous session "because I didn't give you what you wanted about the feelings in my dream. I could tell by your voice." Her therapist replied that he didn't know what his voice was like, but noted that how she experienced it is important. She said, "I was aware of trying to please you, so I tried harder. It's always that way. I don't know what to do in this room. I look for messages. I'm afraid that I won't want to show the feelings you are trying to get to." The "good girl" or "good boy" will also try to be a "good patient," a major transference resistance to be confronted and explored. Their persona of goodness does not go very deep, however. One way or another, the dark side will be evident. She may dutifully bring in her dreams, but will not work on them herself; she will also deny the validity of the therapist's interpretation if he makes one. In effect, she plays out the theme of "I will pretend to do and be what you want, but in fact, I will defeat you." She does not allow her therapist to have an effect. She renders him powerless. Because she envies the power he has, power she is not allowed to have, she spoils it so he will no longer be enviable. Acting out this transference resistance, she sabotages the possibility of her being helped by him. Confrontation and interpretation of the acting out is essential to the dissolution of the impasse.

THE MASOCHISTIC PERSONALITY DISORDER: A DIAGNOSIS WORTH KEEPING

I believe it is unfortunate that *masochistic personality disorder* has been eliminated from the *Diagnostic and Statistical Manual of Mental Disorders*. It has its place in what I view as a family of disorders, the members of which fall along a common developmental track. They are the paranoid personality disorder, the narcissistic personality disorder, and the masochistic personality disorder. I see each as arising at a different point along the developmental continuum. Because there will also be a difference in the core relationship problem, there will be a difference in the nature of the resistances encountered in their treatment as well. Character resistances will protect the structural dangers of those derailed earlier. Transference resistance will be more prominent, with problems amenable to interpretation arising later on the continuum. Each of these disorders is characterized by a history of a significantly salient if not predominant negative or hurtful caretaking environment. The later the derailment, the more positive elements from earlier stages will contribute to the overall picture.

The *paranoid personality disorder* has at its core a salient persecutory object and victim-self alongside an anaclitically depressed objectless self. It is set in motion in the first year of life. Because critical organization processes ought to take place in the first year of life, the effects of gross environmental failures or assaults during this period are the most severe and are basic to personality formation and disorder. The propensity for a psychotic transference is great. Insofar as the primary object relationship is in largest measure persecutory, attempts to connect with the therapist will be based on reenacting the paranoid theme. There will be a major resistance to seeing any attempts of the therapist to be "good" in a positive light, insofar as the patient will experience it as a failure of the therapist to connect with him or her. Paradoxically, when the therapist is good, she is experienced as bad, and when the therapist is perceived as bad, she is experienced as good. This resistance protects the patient from loss of the internal object and descent into anaclitic depression, so the difficulty of such work cannot be overemphasized. It is not work that every therapist will find tolerable or even possible, and it would be folly for many, if not most, therapists to undertake treatment of this patient. Several therapists in my consultation groups were severely stressed—perhaps traumatized—by attempting this work and were helped to find a way to refer the patient.

I see the *narcissistic personality disorder* as arising in the second year, with the onset of the rapprochement phase of development. It reflects the inability of the child to bring together into a single representation the images of the object who is experienced as alternately good or bad. That is, parental inconsistency (usually as a result of the intense ambivalence of the parent toward the young child, or reflecting the parent's personality disorder) is so chronic and so emotionally traumatic that the child at this age is cognitively unable to bring the separate object-images into a single, albeit ambivalently, loved other. The omnipotent grandiose self derives from the infantile omnipotence of the preseparation and individuation stage, and is elaborated through language and consolidated around the defining trait at the center of the grandiosity. It serves as a defensive fallback structure when the good object is disappointing and is devalued and discarded. Kohut (1971) describes this transference dynamic that shifts from an idealizing transference to rageful devaluation of the object and the mobilization of the grandiose self. What distinguishes this splitting is that it is evidence of a developmental failure to integrate for the child what was unintegratable. The split we see in the masochistic personality who was derailed further along the developmental continuum is a defense against the intolerable conflict of an intense ambivalence. In the narcissistic personality, we may see the further regression to a paranoid structure when the grandiose self is challenged by adversity or by a therapist's failure to understand its defensive importance. We need to recall Kohut's reference to the *nonspecific* resistances of this patient by which he maintains his self-cohesion.

The relationship with the primary caretaker may become overly conflicted as the child proceeds further along the developmental continuum to the third year of life. When there is a combination of highly gratifying interactions and highly frustrating or hurtful ones, the child attempts to come to grips with an intense ambivalence, the conflict between love and hate toward the object. I see this failure of the caretakers to support the child's growing individuality and psychological autonomy as the masochist's point of derailment, the point at which the *masochistic personality disorder* arises. Hostility toward, rejection of, or emotional abandonment of the little person the child is becoming leads to defenses and adaptations in the child that preserve loving affect toward the object and protect the object from the rage and hatred that is felt from the negative side of the ambivalence. The dark side goes underground. This is the core relationship problem for this patient. And it forms the nexus of the transference resistance in treatment.

THE MASOCHISTIC PERSONALITY
AND TRANSFERENCE RESISTANCE

Historically, it has been assumed that the masochistic personality takes pleasure in suffering, a gratification that comes from the id. This view was based in instinct theory. In her classic article, "On Teasing and Being Teased: And the Problem of 'Moral Masochism,'" Brenman (1952) notes the difficulty of bringing clinical data together with a coherent theory of psychological organization. She says this is particularly true when the behavior under discussion is "a complex configuration resulting from the interplay of: (1) primitive unconscious drives with (2) defensive processes and (3) adaptive implementations" (264). However, she does touch on interpersonal aspects of the syndrome in her report of a patient who

maintained an unyielding wide-eyed expression of "please-don't-hit-me" and would regularly spring to her feet like a jack-in-the-box in a caricature of deference if the examiner had occasion to rise during the interview. Gradually her own therapist and to some degree other staff members began to tease her. . . . It was as if everyone felt in her unprovoked look of terror and pleading, an unjustified accusation of evil intent and an undefined implicit demand. (266)

Today, we speak of such events in the treatment situation as enactments in which the early self and object-relationship conflict is replayed with the unconscious collusion of the therapist. Therapists have reported a felt inclination to play out this projective identification with patients like this. Their own latent sadism threatens to be activated.

If we reassess this pattern of behavior from an interpersonal, object-relational perspective, we find that the reinforcing gratification comes from a grandiose, perfectionistic ego-ideal. "I will not stoop to his level." Translated, this says, "I am morally superior." This shift makes clinging to the role of victim analyzable as a transference resistance. I have heard analysts who speak of this kind of gratification as an "addiction" and, as such, unanalyzable. They are in, effect, viewing it from the older perspective of the instinctual pleasure seated in the id.

Brenman, in keeping with instinct theory, says that the complex and infinitely toned varieties of masochistic formations express "simultaneously the unusually strong need and the consequent aggression when this need is frustrated in fact or fantasy" (273). This brings us to the developmental continuum and the relationship set-up within which this need was manifest and within which it became problematic.

Brenman also emphasizes the use of projective mechanisms for masochistic formations, saying that the masochistic individual is ready to feel exploited by virtue of his projection of his own exploitativeness. He also projects his own hate-filled envy and becomes fearful of the envy of the other toward him. The more he sabotages his own goals so that the other will not envy him, the more he envies the other.

Furthermore, shame is felt as a result of taking on the devalued position vis-à-vis the powerful object. As a defense against this shame, the patient has recourse to her secret superiority, usually moral. The associated contempt for the other who buys into the consciously played out self-effacing posture, along with the compensatory moral superiority, can be viewed as analogous to the devalued object-grandiose-self shift observed in the case of the narcissistic personality disorder. The self-effacing behaviors and the claims of unimpeachable goodness are manifestations of reaction formation.

There is, in the adult, a double projection. First she projects the narcissistic and rageful object into the other and then relates in a manner to appease and placate that person. Then her own repressed narcissistic rage, evoked by feeling forced to deny herself in the service of the other, is also projected. With both, she caters to the narcissism she has attributed to the other, so the other will not turn against her. Then there is further resentment at being the one sacrificed to the wishes and demands of the other. It is a vicious circle that feeds on itself. It is in this piece of the circle—her own denied and projected rage, her dark side—that we can see the familial resemblance to the narcissistic personality disorder. Sometimes the angry feelings of entitlement to compensation for the self-sacrifice may come out in the form of stealing. She feels perversely justified and without guilt. The masochistic personality has one foot in the pre-Oedipal stage and the other in the Oedipal stage, and may often be seen as more evolved than she is. Nevertheless, the relationship advancement to the capacity for ambivalence and associated cognitive achievements in this individual make it more possible for us to do straightforward interpretive work than in the more primitive constellations. Even when getting to the dark side, the therapeutic alliance is not damaged, and the observing ego can be relied on in the work.

The British physician and journalist Anthony Daniels (2001) reports on the view that, for some, anger is its own justification. The person with a grievance who considers himself a victim "can do no wrong. Normal moral constraints do not apply to the enraged, because rage is inherently generous and holy." He sees this righting of a grievance, real or imagined, as the nearest many people can come nowadays to a transcendent purpose in life. It is no surprise that what has become a cultural shift toward moral masochism and its attitude of victimhood is met so frequently in the clinical situation.

What I have observed clinically is the overarching importance of preserving an image of the self as good. This can be seen as a perversion of the ego-ideal, which, along with conscience, is part of the superego. With a healthy ego-ideal, a person has a well-established sense of himself or herself as a worthwhile person. A healthy ego-ideal is realistic. The individual's image of himself does not require unrealistic perfection or reveal grandiosity.

So where does the anger and its hurtful aggression go? There may be this transformation of what is bad—that is, the more primitive hate and rage—into a morally justified, self-righteous position, the anger rising in the form of righteous indignation. A view of oneself as an innocent victim becomes solidified. Enormous emotion and energy can be mobilized around social or political causes. Displaced in this way, hostile and even violent aggression can be morally justified. A man who had been terribly abused by his father throughout childhood nevertheless led an outwardly moral and good life. Yet he yearned to be able to fight in a "just war," where his wish to kill would not only be sanctioned, but rewarded, perhaps with a medal for bravery. He knitted the hate and rage he felt toward his father together with his strong conscience.

The therapist can get caught up in an unconscious collusion if he or she shares similar values with respect to the patient's pet social or political cause. A loss of neutrality will cause him to be blind to the resistance aspect of the patient's devotion to the cause. The patient convinces the therapist that he is a good and noble person, not wanting her to see the dark side that lurks just beneath the surface. A countertransference resistance will join with the transference resistance to form an impasse in the treatment process.

INHIBITIONS RESULTING FROM RENUNCIATION OF HEALTHY AGGRESSION

In the sexual realm, the active thrusting of the male partner requires access to healthy aggression. If he has buried that aspect of his personality along with the denial of his dark side, he may develop the symptom of impotence or, even more profoundly, inhibition of sexual desire. Sometimes this individual may report to his therapist that he is at his most potent when he is angry at his partner. In this case, his hostile aggression is released and, with it, his bottled up potency. Angry sex seems to be the best he can do. "Making love" for the man requires access to his healthy, nonhostile aggression. Some men report that they compensate for this inhibition by indulging in secret hostility-laden aggressive fantasies while they are supposedly "making love."

While the woman can be completely passive and receptive in intercourse, her active participation in reaching toward her mate is more likely to enhance her own pleasure as well as his. This, too, requires that same access to healthy aggression.

Successful participation in competitive sports requires the same access to healthy aggression. An unconscious guilt about all aggression that has been repressed as part of the dark side will often lead to an automatic self-sabotage when the individual is in danger of winning. Needing only one point to win the tennis match, invariably he will hit what would have been the perfect shot, straight into the net. "Good boys" and "good girls" pay a price in many arenas of life in the service of preserving their morally superior self-image.

GENDER DIFFERENCES

I have observed that, in the therapy situation, there are more "good girls" than "good boys." That doesn't mean that good boys have not been found.

What seems to be a common situation is that in which the individual, as a child (and later, too) stays overly close to his mother, adapting to her needs and expectations. When he does rebel, it tends to be in secret; he hides his bad-boy self from her (as he will from his therapist later on). In effect, he does an end-run around his conscience. He smokes and reads pornography in his hideaway. As an adult, after his wife has gone to sleep, he sneaks down to his computer and logs on to his favorite porn site.

By virtue of their gender, boys are less likely to stay stuck in this kind of relationship with the mother. It will make him feel like a sissy; his sense of maleness is endangered. He will push away from her just to confirm his boy-ness to himself. When little boys compete to see who can pee the farthest, they confirm their gender as well as their separateness and differentness from mother.

While it may be easier to grow up female because gender is firmly established early on, it is also easier for girls to get stuck in their mother's orbit. Being good—adapting to mother's expectations and demands—is believed essential to ensure mother's love. Yet simmering hatreds and resentments remain buried or hidden. Self-imposed frustration of goals and ambitions later in life reinforces these feelings. One can expect that this way of relating will be reenacted as a transference resistance.

Uncovering the demons and monsters, however, is essential to a good therapeutic outcome. The capacity for healthy, self-assertive, goal-oriented behavior inevitably will be tied to what is repressed. Desire and will belong to the repressed and frustrated self. This exploration is not likely to be without high levels of anxiety and guilt, and will be the most strongly resisted in the work. It brings both the patient and the therapist face-to-face with the repressed parental imago and the hostile feelings and impulses associated with it.

Analytic therapy will have to address the core relationship conflict and the flight from ambivalence. Because the developmental stage of emotional derailment is later than it is for the paranoid personality disorder or the narcissistic personality disorder, we do not run into the same difficulties as we have in the work with the more primitive character structure. Despite the expected defenses and resistances, there is a cohesive self and the availability of an observing ego on which to rely. For example, the patient's unwavering pleasantness toward the therapist and attempts to be helpful—manifestations of the transference resistance—will have to be juxtaposed with the subtle or not-so-subtle indications of the other side of the coin.

The next chapter addresses another powerful resistance to the work of therapy: the sexualization of the core relationship problem. Once again, the point of emotional, psychological derailment is central to the problem. Deciphering the compromise formation brought about by the psyche-soma link is essential for the work to progress.

5

The Sexualization of the Core Relationship Problem as Resistance

THE PSYCHE–SOMA LINK

Joyce McDougall (1974), exploring the intricate and inevitable connection of psyche and soma, describes how in the case of the conversion symptoms of hysteria, *"the body lends itself and its functions to the mind to use as the mind wills"* (italics added). Nowhere can this be better illustrated than the various ways in which sexuality and the core relationship conflicts come together.

The classical understanding of the *compromise formation* is that it is an idea or an act that substitutes for and represents all sides of a repressed conflict. It creatively weaves together the separate elements of the conflict within an apparently cohesive whole. Its very usefulness in reducing felt dissonance reinforces its power. For example, in conceptualizing sexual perversion in Freudian terms, Stoller (1975) writes that the ego creates a "compromise formation that will (partially) gratify the instinctual wish while placating the superego or reality demands that the wish be gone" (93).

If we think of this substitution as encompassing the various elements of the core relationship conflict, rather than balancing id, ego, and superego forces, analysis of the compromise formation will elucidate the conflict and make it accessible to the analytic work. A particularly powerful compromise formation is that of the sexual fantasy. Whatever the down side of living in fantasy, the illusion of total control over all the characters and events is enormously reassuring and gratifying. The individual writes the script. He casts the roles. There is nothing in his fantasy that he does not want there. Everything serves a psychological purpose for him. The hold these fantasies have on the individual is magnified many times over because of the added element of sexual pleasure or release. The sexual fantasy is more obviously interpersonal in nature, even when there is no one else in the room.

As a powerful biological drive, sex has the ability to *capture* early unarticulated relationship conflicts, and sexual fantasies will then be a way for the individual to both symbolize and manage conflicts that he might not be able to articulate. Beliefs about one's self, about the other, and about the nature of interpersonal relationships are woven together into one story, with sexual arousal and desire added to the mix.

The eroticization of the psychological conflict embedded in the compromise formation creates a psyche–soma link that contributes further to the power of the compromise formation as a solution. Focused genital awareness and conscious awareness of sexuality come about in the early years of life, especially between two and four, but afterward as well. This conscious focus differs from any earlier bodily sensations of pleasure at times of stimulation, such as when the baby is being cleaned by his caretaker. This new awareness is a powerful biological and physical force and it is drawn to another powerful psychological force. This other force is the most central, salient, and significant relationship pattern of the child's existence at the time of emergence of this focused genital sexuality. In this way, the relationship scenario that we might say is on the front burner of the child's awareness and concern—whether it is positive or negative—and sexuality come together like two pieces of Velcro. This union will reveal itself directly or indirectly in what "turns a person on" later in life. That is, it has been rendered erotic. For example, if the core relationship problem is one of an insecure attachment coupled with the individual's attempts to find ways to control or possess the object, this theme will run through his sexual fantasies.

In his classic study of murderers, Bjerre ([1927] 1981) describes their hate: "It was the hate of the weak, suffering, and incompetent for all strong, happy, self-assured persons: it grew out of fear and envy, and in the last resort out of a sense of helplessness and inferiority." Bjerre conveys how their sexuality could not be tied to any conception of love. Of one notorious killer, he writes: "His pleasure in every new sexual connection was based on the imaginary belief that his mistress of the moment was completely in his power and that she must yield, even to the point of death, to his all conquering whims" (117). Although the patient reporting fantasies of this nature may not go to the extent of acting them out in reality, they will reveal a similar core relationship problem.

This view of the coming together of two separate lines of development is consistent with Anna Freud's (1965) concept of *developmental lines*. This concept explains how pathology can result from a failure in normal human development in one or more areas of growth. Each line of development charts the emergence of a specific developmental potential through a sequence of stages of growth.

In her review of the work of Wrye and Welles (1994) on the *maternal erotic transference*, Person (1997) notes an example of the coming together of object relations development and the emergence of genital sexuality. Person criticizes what she describes as the authors' "collapsing sex and bonding into an undifferentiated 'erotic' transference" (269). I agree with Person when she describes the "closely intertwined (but still separate) developmental lines for attunement and attachment, on the one hand, and for sexuality, on the other" (270). Although communication may be transmitted through bodily feelings and sensations, it is the impairments in the processes of bonding and attachment that constitute the core relationship problem and are clinically relevant and interpretable.

While Horney (1950) does not write in terms of object relations theory, she does examine the connection between "sexual desire" and "love" in her own terms. Her use of the word "love" is broad and vague and muddies the specifics of the nature of the relationship in question. However, she does make note of what happens to the sex/relationship connection in what she refers to as the neuroses. She writes: "Sexuality retains in neuroses the functions it naturally has as a means of physical satisfaction and of intimate human contact. Also sexual well-functioning adds in many ways to the feeling of self-confidence. But in neuroses all these functions are enlarged and take on a different coloring. Sexual activities become not only a release of sexual tensions but also of manifold nonsexual tensions" (301).

Horney approaches a projective identification view when she writes, "He may talk about some weakness in himself which he profoundly despises, and have sadistic fantasies of torturing somebody weaker than he is." This can also be seen as an "identification with the aggressor."

She notes further that: "Sexual functioning, being attractive or desirable, the choice of a partner, the quantity or variety of sexual experiences—all become a matter of pride more than of wishes and enjoyment. The more the personal factor in love relations recedes and the purely sexual ones ascend, the more does the unconscious concern about lovableness shift to a conscious concern about attractiveness" (302). That is, in terms of the core relationship problem, the preoccupation about sexual desirability will be a resistance to uncovering the core issue of an insecure attachment with the primary object.

Horney foreshadows McDougall saying, "Sexuality is put in the service of neurotic needs. For this reason it often assumes an *undue* importance, in the sense of an importance stemming from non-sexual sources."

WORKING WITH THE SEXUAL FANTASY

Because the patient views his fantasy as the key to sexual expression and gratification, he or she may be reluctant to bring it into question in treatment. He doesn't want it taken away by analysis. When this is the case, a major resistance to the work itself arises. It becomes a transference resistance when concern for the therapist's response to hearing the fantasy also comes into play. Furthermore, the issue is joined by a countertransference resistance when the therapist's discomfort with addressing sexual matters leads to his or her avoidance of the subject. In my consultation groups, I heard cases in which resistance to the therapy, transference resistance, and countertransference resistance came together to prevent progress in the treatment, often for many years.

There are many examples of sexual fantasies central to the compromise formation. For example, if the most significant and salient pattern for the individual's core relationship pattern engendered hurt and endangered feelings, sexual fantasies later on may dramatize scenarios of hurting and being hurt. Hurting and being hurt became eroticized. In the fantasy, the roles may be switched although the relationship drama is the same. The dynamic of projective identification is operative in this dual-role assignment. Feelings of powerlessness and shame may alternate with a sense of power and arrogant pride. The man with fantasies of being tortured might never risk looking for an actual partner with whom to enact his scenarios. His survival instinct and good judgment stop him from taking such a chance. In his fantasy, the power he has over the hurtful other acts as an antidote to feelings of powerlessness and shame. In addition, the ability to bear the pain inflicted on him in the fantasy creates an illusion of strength and feelings of pride that counteract the weakness and shame of submission. In some cases, we may learn that the strict father used his belt to discipline his young son. Perhaps bearing the pain without crying when his father beat him made him feel powerful and proud, as it now does in his fantasy encounters. He is likely to boast, "He couldn't make me cry." In his fantasies, there may be pleasure in the power he experiences in frustrating his tormentor by withholding the response he wanted to elicit. This same pleasure in frustrating the therapist's attempts to have him confront the painful memories with their associated fear and rage may constitute the essence of a transference resistance. Although the fantasies are sexual in nature, the fundamental relational conflict of power and submission will be reenacted in the treatment relationship in a variety of ways. The issue of where this person was derailed from the developmental continuum will be especially important, although the therapist may neglect to make this determination, assuming the belt-wielding father was at the center of the patient's difficulties. Was the issue of domination and submission central to his mother's reactions to his attempts to individuate and establish autonomy? If so, the treatment will have to move in that direction because of the characterological implications and the transference resistances that may relate to that earlier core relationship problem.

If the major resistances have been addressed and treatment continues to progress, the core relationship problem will have been elucidated. Its resolution will now have moved into the working-through stage of therapy. At this time, reemergence of the fantasy and any impulse to act on it become increasingly dystonic or ego-alien. Now, recognizing its defensive or compensatory functions in the original compromise formation, and exploring what was going on before its reemergence, will be part of the working through process. What is usually found is a reexperiencing of the core relationship conflict in present-day life, whether it be in the world of work, in a close interpersonal relationship, or even in the transference.

ACTING OUT AS A RESISTANCE

Acting out in reality is a patient's use of particular behaviors in place of actually recalling memories that are too painful to remember. It is a substitute for verbal symbolization and, therefore, a resistance to doing the work of therapy. Persistent acting out indicates a deeper, untouched, or unresolved conflict. It is an attempt to make the fantasy real. Because it provides a temporary *solution* rather than a resolution, its value wears off before long and the individual returns to the same behavior over and over. Because of this repetitive pattern, it is sometimes diagnosed as an obsessive-compulsive disorder. Remembering that the obsessive-compulsive behavior pattern is a defense mechanism used to protect the individual from the distress of a core relationship problem rather than a disease in and of itself will immunize the therapist from becoming co-opted by a medical model and abandoning a psychology of the mind.

The anxiety of an insecure gender identity in some men frequently leads to acting out behavior that temporarily relieves that anxiety. For example, such a patient may be heterosexual, perhaps married, but may find himself drawn to promiscuous, anonymous sex with men in the baths. His anxiety is heightened by his fear of contracting AIDS. A therapist who rushes to judgment and declares the patient to be defending against homosexuality will make a grave error. This is a good example of where the diagnosis often cannot be made on the basis of the presenting problem.

With respect to the biologically normal male child—and it is important to note that those cases of biologically determined gender disorders are relatively rare—both parents play critical roles in the achievement of a secure male gender identity. This core gender identity is the person's *self-designation* as male or female.

Although the mother may be able to provide a secure symbiosis, she must also be psychologically ready to *release him from it* in a stage-appropriate manner, to support his separation from her. Then she has to support his individuation with the unfolding of his uniqueness, which includes his maleness and his little-boy behavior. That is, she does not need to have his behavior conform to her idea of what a good child should be when this image has no room for an intrinsic true boy-self. Teachers of the early grades often have a punitive attitude toward the noisy or motor-driven behaviors of the little boys in their classrooms. In this manner, the wider culture often exerts overly restrictive constraints on the maleness of the young boy. It becomes equated with badness.

The good-enough mother values maleness in general and in her son in particular. She does not overvalue it, which may lead to her envy of it and a need to destroy it. Nor does she wish for a daughter in his place, needing to erase his maleness in the service of her wish-fulfilling fantasies. In sum, she is truly happy to have a son and so takes pleasure in his unfolding as a boy with an identity of his own, and this includes his gender identity. Her failure to do so may cause developmental derailment during the separation–individuation process. The core relationship problem will be manifest later in life in his way of being in the world. While a little girl faced with the same stage of derailment will have other problems, an insecure gender identity is not likely to be one of them. It is for this reason that most gender identity disorders occur in males (Greenson 1968).

The father plays a complementary role. Loeb and Shane (1982) note that the absent or detached father "does not allow the male child to identify with him, and thus use him as a bridge to achieve both an individual sense of self and a gender identity" as a male (423). Overall, the good-enough father offers the love and support that facilitates the boy's ability to move away from mother, to know that there is love and support other than what she provides. He may be able to counteract tendencies on her part to hold on to her young son for her own psychological reasons. He doesn't envy his son nor does he have to destroy the boy's emerging maleness because of his own competitive or envious dynamic. He must also provide a model that the boy can identify with while still feeling good about himself. In some instances in which the father's maleness was manifest in hurtful and frightening aggression, the son may say, "I didn't want to be like him. I hated the way he was." That is, there was a refusal to identify with the father in order to maintain a sense of congruence with the ego-ideal. If the father, on the other hand, is perceived as weak or ineffectual and the mother is viewed as the holder of strength and power, the son will be reluctant to give up the identification with her and coun-teridentify with the father. To do so would render him vulnerable to be-ing shamed or humiliated. In these situations, the boy may have emerged from the primary identification with mother but then may have formed a secondary identification, a reidentification, with her in the service of the ego-ideal.

Lidz and Lidz (1986) have brought the issue of male gender identity de-velopment to our attention from an anthropological perspective. In Papua New Guinea, where boys lived with the women until the age of six and then moved to where the men lived, harsh rituals were carried out in or-der to wipe out the boy's primary identification with his mother and forcefully initiate a firm male identity. These rituals made concrete that which we speak of in mental terms. Papua New Guinea natives would forcefully bleed the little boy from the nose to rid him of mother's femaleness. They then would carry out ritual fellatio in order to infuse maleness. The boys thus were inseminated via the man's penis in order to become men. It is not surprising that they became fierce warriors!

One patient reported fantasies of being overcome by a powerful man and anally penetrated, reaming out what did not belong there along with an infusion of what was needed. The patient who came to therapy re-porting his secret trips to the baths where this fantasy was acted out did not have a sexual problem. He had a gender identity problem directly re-lated to the core relationship problem and his derailment from the devel-opmental continuum during the separation and individuation period. This was where the therapy had to go. Issues of individuation would be played out as transference resistance in the treatment.

Countertransference resistances may come into play with a female ther-apist. In my view, a female therapist with both an intellectual under-standing of male development and a genuine attitude of appreciation of maleness can work as successfully with a man with compromised gender identity as can a male therapist. This attitude of appreciation has to be free of any tendency to idealize maleness or eroticize the power attributed to maleness (as we might find in a woman with unresolved Oedipal issues). She also has to be free of any envy of the position and power accorded to men in her family of origin or in society as a whole. Whatever the female therapist's failure to appreciate the importance of gender and male po-tency issues or even to hear them in the material, she may do a disservice to some of her male patients. The actual work is done through an em-pathic understanding that is *communicated through interpretation*. I want to emphasize that her stance is an analytic one, not one of a woman admir-ing a man (as one student interpreted my remarks.)

Countertransference resistances may be based on sexual politics in which either an affirmation of female power or a unisex approach to social–sexual issues leads to a denial or dismissal of these critical issues of men as having their own importance. One can support efforts to achieve equal pay for equal work or confront the realities of the so-called glass ceiling in the corporate world without allowing these convictions to create generalized and negative attitudes toward men and all things male. An antipathy toward anything deemed "macho" may lead to an unconscious countertransference reinforcement of early maternal devaluation of male-associated behaviors and maternal undercutting of the young son's true self-expression of those behaviors.

This chapter has described clinical examples of how the sexualization of the core relationship problem can stand as a very difficult transference resistance. It is made even more difficult when the patient's acting-out creates another resistance to the very fabric of analytic psychotherapy. It is also an example of how complex these issues can be and how difficult the work can be for the therapist who loses sight of the heart of the problem.

The next chapter addresses the issue of how the need or wish for power can become a resistance in psychotherapy. If one cannot find emotional security or extract love by being good in the other's eyes, maybe that person can gain control over the needed other and obtain security in that way.

6

The Wish for Power
as a Resistance

The role of power in human motivation and behavior is seriously un-
appreciated and underestimated. Nietzsche concluded that the will to
power was *the* primary motivational force. He believed that although people claimed that what they wanted most in life was happiness, in reality
what they wanted most was power.

Although we need not accept Nietzsche's views as definitive of the human species, we would do well to keep in mind his observation that the
wish for power does pervade all aspects of human behavior. In therapy,
power issues need to be identified, made explicit, and understood in
terms of how power is used to compensate for and defend against the
anxiety and shame of powerlessness. With this knowledge, power as an
issue can be separated out from whatever else in going on in a relationship. As with the sexual fantasy, the core relationship problem in which
the felt need for power is embedded must become the organizing principle for the work of analytic psychotherapy. Power as a motivating force
will inevitably interfere with the ability to construct and move toward
healthy and gratifying goals.

The wish for power may be second only to the need for love, and the two
often go together. In some cases, the need for power is primary. In its benev-
olent form, particularly in the case of parents, power affords us leadership,
protection, and security. In its malevolent form, it brings domination or
abuse. The power differential characterizing the relationship between a parent and a young child is the first and most formative experience with this in-
escapable dimension of life and of all subsequent interpersonal relationships.
This includes the relationship with a psychotherapist, where the defensive or

compensatory need for power will become a major source of resistance. To the extent that this includes power over the therapist, it is a transference resistance. If the need for power permeates all aspects of life, we will view it as characterological and, thus, probably as a character resistance.

Family therapist Jay Haley (1969) observed the dynamics of power in the troubled families who came to him for help. He writes:

> Power tactics are those maneuvers a person uses to give himself influence and control over his social world and so to make the world more predictable . . . a man has power if he can order someone to behave in a certain way, but he also has power if he can provoke someone to behave in that way. . . . Many individuals appear to consider the gain of power positions more important than any subjective distress they might experience. (6)

Our attitude toward early experiences with primary caretakers determines how we use our own later power (or how we refuse to use it), and how we react to the power of others—whether we seek it and cling to it, hiding behind it for safety, whether we hate and envy it, wanting to destroy it, or whether we rebel against it, overtly or covertly. All of these styles of managing power dynamics may be brought into treatment and played out with the therapist. If the therapist is not able to understand the defensive and compensatory strategies of the patient's behavior, countertransference reactions may then become a countertransference resistance. An entrenched power struggle, overt or covert, may be set in play, with progress in treatment stopped in its tracks.

Power and aggression are not the same. They are subjectively and experientially different from one another. People may not say they feel good when they are being aggressive. Indeed, they may feel conflicted and guilty. They will, however, say they feel good when they can experience themselves as powerful. They may even bear the guilt that comes from feeling aggressive in order to feel powerful. They may also bear the shame of powerlessness in order to not be aggressive.

KINDS OF POWER (HORNER 1989)

Intrinsic power

What I refer to as "intrinsic power" refers to a sense of mastery, competency, and potency in one's dealings with the world of things and with the world of people. There is a sense of being effective, of having an impact, of mattering. It is the power to think, to feel, to know—to experience the creative workings of the mind. It is the power that comes with access to one's own will, with a secure sense of self, of one's legitimate place in the world, and in one's relationships. It is a sense of being a grown-up in a world of grown-ups and of knowing that the only secret is that there is no secret.

Those who fully and without conflict experience their intrinsic power have their feet planted firmly in reality, in contrast to those who try to live out a fantasy existence of illusion—of grandiosity and omnipotence that cover up an underlying sense of worthlessness and helplessness. Real intrinsic power transcends the whim of chance or of fortune, enabling the individual to persevere and even triumph through adversity. It is what the words of the poem *Invictus* imply: "I am the master of my fate/I am the captain of my soul." They do not imply claims of omnipotence, but of the intrinsic power to play the hand one is dealt with integrity and authenticity.

The threads of will and power are closely intertwined, and the term "willpower" reveals the intuitive understanding of their linkage. The third thread is that of aggression, which, as we have seen, may complicate issues of will and power. The *feeling* of having power, as a feeling, belongs to the realm of the emotions, although it is often experienced at the bodily level as well. More precisely, the *emotion* that goes with the *experience* of power is likely to be *elation*, a kind of "high." Carried to a pathological extreme, this would become the high of the manic state, with its associated sense of omnipotence. Having a sense of mastery and competence not only makes a person feel good about himself or herself, which is essentially a judgment and an enhanced self-esteem—it also *feels* good in and of itself.

Will is more closely tied to what is referred to as "intentionality," and it has a cognitive or ideational component. To say, "I intend to do such and such," implies the will to do it. It is something one can articulate with words, that one can think about. It is a course of action decided on and the determination to see it through. Will is an attribute of the self determined to express or assert its own nature. The sense of mastery that comes from the successful expression of will leads to the feeling referred to here as "intrinsic power." Obviously, for one to live in society, will has to be tempered not only with reality-testing and judgment, but also with concern for others and for society itself. Some parents see in this a necessity to "break the child's will" at that point of development when it comes more clearly into conflict with the wishes of the parents. Unfortunately, to break the child's will is to break the child. Becoming derailed from the developmental continuum at this point will leave the individual with a core relationship problem in which these issues are embedded. The struggle will emerge in therapy as an acting-out or as a transference resistance.

Will may be subjected to repression and inhibition when it is suffused with anger and experienced as an act *against* the other. A young man was struggling to find not only his sense of who he was, his identity, but also to re-find the intrinsic power that seemed to have been lost earlier in life. He told his therapist:

> I have to use my strength against my parents to be a man, to make an independent decision. When I make a decision they lose control of my life. It shows I'm not an outgrowth of them. Sometimes all this makes me feel guilty. When I expressed my own feelings as a child, I was put down. Now a war has to be fought to get my feelings out. I'm impressed with some of the things I get done. My power blows me away. The more powerless I feel, the more excited I become when I *do* feel powerful.

In addition to facing up to the origins of the paralysis in his life, he had to confront the ways in which he sabotaged himself in order not to challenge his parents' power.

The patient may submit to what he perceives as the will of the therapist. As noted previously, Friedman (1997) refers to the *demand structure of the treatment,* observing that "if you don't offer one demand, the patient will perceive another" (29). The perceived demand will derive from the conscious or unconscious expectations inherent in the core relationship problem. An example of perceived demand is that he, the patient, must be responsive to the narcissistic vulnerabilities he has attributed to his therapist; that, as with his mother, he must never upset the therapist; and that the therapist's wish to help him must be bought at a price to the self. The patient will relate to the therapist in adapting to these perceived demands just as he adapted to his mother as a child. This, of course, will constitute a transference resistance.

The patient may submit to what he sees as the will of the therapist. Subtle manifestations of this must be picked up at once and addressed by the therapist. He might say, "I have been noticing that when I say something or am about to say something, you immediately defer to me rather than following your own line of thought. What do you think this is all about?"

On the other hand, the patient may feel the need to assert his will, even when it patently makes no sense. The therapist may express his puzzlement about this bit of acting out. My favorite model for this style of inquiry is the television detective Columbo. "I'm really puzzled. Can you help me understand what was going on when you did that?" In his very manner of inquiry, the therapist does not "steal" the patient's power, thus intensifying the transference resistance or the acting-out.

In its purest sense, aggression is merely an impulse toward action. The child may have the will, or intention, of reaching out for a nearby toy. The *act* of reaching for it is a manifestation of his healthy aggression, his ability to *go toward* the aim of his intent. A positive marriage of will and aggression is necessary for a person to be effective in the world.

If one is frightened by his or her own impulse toward some action, especially when there is anger or rage behind it, or feels guilty because of the nature of the motive behind it, he or she may guard against such an impulse by repudiating intention, by denying the wish, and by inhibiting the will. The "good boy" or "good girl" will be subject to this way of being. Feelings of powerlessness and anxiety will be a consequence of these inhibitions, and with them self-esteem and self-respect suffer. The pride of intrinsic power gives way to shame of its absence. This is not to imply that it is desirable to act on every impulse. What is desired is an adequate knowledge about one's own perhaps hidden conflicts and motives so that, rather than simply renouncing or inhibiting will, one is able to make conscious choices based on judgment and values.

Intrinsic power has three facets, which can best be stated in terms of "I am," "I can," and "I will." To put it in another way, it is in terms of *identity*, *mastery*, and *intentionality*. People who do not have a sense of their own identity may report that they do *not* know what they want—that they feel as though they have no will of their own. Distortions of identity lead to a loss of intrinsic power. It may be replaced by illusory power that is destructive in its expression, or that becomes essential as a protection against a terrifying awareness of the fragility of helplessness that goes with a poorly defined identity. In this situation, clinging to the illusory power is a character resistance, the defensive functions of which need to be understood by the therapist.

It should be evident that we must determine where the individual with difficulties in one or more sectors of intrinsic power was derailed from the developmental continuum and what the residual core relationship problem may be. It will be brought into psychotherapy where, sooner or later and in one way or another, it will be played out in the transference and show up as a transference resistance. With the developmental perspective and the core relationship problem as an organizing principle of the clinical material, the dynamics of these various and complex threads of the individual's way of being in the world will be made clear. What we should do in the clinical situation will also be clearer to us.

Attributed Power

People often bring their dependency needs or wishes into their intimate adult relationships. This is particularly true with the spouse who may be experienced as having power over oneself, just as though the spouse were a parent. It is especially true with the psychotherapist. In the language of psychoanalysis, this attribution is what we call "transference." As we know, exploring therapeutic interaction enables an individual to understand how he or she transfers into current adult relationships the feelings, beliefs, wishes, or fears—as well as strategies for managing relationships with significant others—from the formative relationships of childhood. It also enables the individual to learn how these feelings, beliefs, wishes, and fears came to be built into his or her adult character and how they are now central to the very problems that bring him or her into therapy. This is the essence of the treatment process. Bromberg (1996) notes that we do not try to cure people of what happened to them. We try to cure them of what they now do to themselves and others in order to cope with what happened to them. From these maladaptive patterns of life we will be able to pull out the underlying wishes and fears with respect to interpersonal relationships and identify them as a resistance when they are played out with the therapist.

On the other hand, power may be arrogated to the self in an equally unrealistic manner. Delusions of grandeur are an obvious and extreme example of this. When parental power is felt to be malevolent, the child may hold on to an illusory omnipotence as a basis of security. More subtle and more common are secret, hidden beliefs about a powerful self who needs nothing from anyone else, a stance assisted by convictions of the superior ability, wisdom, or morality of a perfect self. This is acted out in cases of anorexia. The anorectic girl clings to this delusion, even in the face of death. The grandiose self of the narcissistic personality disorder also fits this paradigm. As Kohut cautions us, while this may be a resistance, it is essential for the maintenance of the patient's self-cohesion. We do not challenge it until much, much later in treatment, when there will be sufficient structural change to make the patient able to withstand exploration of his or her grandiosity without falling apart.

Once again, we are reminded of the necessity of determining where on the developmental continuum the person was derailed and what the residual core relationship problem is now if we are to be able to identify the transference resistances and work with them, directly or indirectly.

Formal Power

The objective power of the government or its agents, such as a policeman, or of one's teacher or employer, is referred to as *formal power.* These individuals are designated to be the holders of power by virtue of title or position. The ultimate goals of designated or formal power are to enable a social system to operate in a coordinated manner toward the achievement of shared purposes. The word "anarchy" refers to the absence of any form of political authority and is associated with disorder and confusion. Spinoza noted that we hand over power to a sovereign in return for restraining the anarchy that threatens all possibility of peace and survival. This view of formal power addresses the degree to which it is *designated* and to which it ultimately resides in those who hand it over, a view consistent with a democratic form of government. Those governments whose formal power is also absolute render their citizens powerless, a situation that generates envy and hatred of the state and an inclination to steal or overthrow that power.

In these instances, as is the case of parents and their young children, there will be moral and philosophical issues with respect to the use or abuse of power. How do the power politics of the family affect the development of the child as he or she traverses the developmental tasks from birth on? When parents are unwilling to relinquish their formal power in keeping with the development of their child's intrinsic power, a situation evolves that produces hatred and envy of parental power and the power of others in positions of authority, along with the wish to overthrow it. This rebellion often erupts in adolescence when the innate developmental thrust of that time counteracts the submissiveness of childhood. Too often, the form this rebellion takes is destructive to the girl or boy. Paradoxically, it may also be the only route open to the young person to claim his formerly repressed intrinsic power. Through it, he regains a sense of who he is as a separate self and of his impeded will. Therapists who work with adolescent boys and girls must understand this paradox and help the young person untangle these complex threads. A transference resistance may be set up at the start inasmuch as the teen will see the therapist as another authority figure with whom he will have to fight for his own power. A straightforward elucidation of the bind he is in will help him accept the therapist as someone whose power he can trust. It will be used to help him and not to imprison him.

Speaking on the telephone with a thirteen-year-old girl who was balking at her parents' wish to bring her for treatment, the therapist cut through the resistance by inviting the girl to come in just once and join her for a cup of coffee at the coffee shop next door. She did not invite her to go out for ice cream. As a signifier, the coffee said, "I am treating you as an adult, not as a child." Thus, for the moment, the impasse over the power dimension was dissolved. As a result of the therapist taking this route, the girl agreed to return the following week.

The patient will, willy-nilly, attribute power to the therapist. This is not all in his mind, as the therapist has real, formal power in the situation. He has the power of agreeing or refusing to see the patient. He has the power to say how much the patient must pay, when he must come to his sessions, and when the session must end. He sets the frame. If the therapist is uncomfortable with this reality, he may make misguided attempts to equalize the relationship. In the case of the thirteen-year-old girl, this suggestion of equality was a temporary expedient that allowed the therapy to begin. In the therapist, the attempts to equalize the relationship may come from his unconscious wish to ward off the patient's envious hatred or competitive wish to bring him down. The therapist may justify his position by claiming its moral-philosophical basis. At any rate, he will deny his own power and set in motion a countertransference resistance to the exploration of the power dynamics of the relationship. When it is clear that a power dynamic is in motion, the therapist has to be able to bring up the issue in a neutral manner with the obvious goal of understanding it. He may say, "Yes, that is my policy. Can you tell me what about it is troublesome for you?" This understanding will be rooted in the origins of the issue in the relationships with primary caretakers and manifested in here-and-now interactions.

A teenage boy declared his wish to be a policeman so he could carry a gun and make people do what he wanted them to do. A need for personal power can find a route of formal power in order to express it. Of course, for some people this is a set-up for the abuse of formal power. In the more ordinary situation of day-to-day life, certain kinds of attributed power affect the attitude and behavior of an individual toward the holders of formal power. Anger toward an overbearing father, for example, is transferred inappropriately to one's employer, leading to work difficulties with a failure to succeed on the job. Attributed power carries with it beliefs, emotions, and motives that affect not only relationships with formal authority, but also social and intimate relationships as well.

THE POWER FACTOR ALONG
THE DEVELOPMENTAL CONTINUUM

Preattachment

Fears associated with "flashback" memories of the black hole, the abyss, or nothingness will generate a resistance that might be termed "relationship at any price." Failure of the primary caretaker to provide the presence and continuity to protect the youngest child's "going-on-being," as Winnicott described it, subjects the infant to alternating states of connection—good or bad—and the nothingness of what is recognized in the adult as the anaclitic depression. The patient will anxiously devise a variety of strategies to maintain her connection with the therapist, which may be experienced by the therapist as anxious clinging. They may also be experienced as the patient's attempts to control him or her—which they may indeed be. These would have been strategies the patient devised as motor and language development proceeded as a defense against the terrifying powerlessness of the situation of infancy. These strategies must be understood as character resistance, insofar as they are felt to be necessary for survival—for going-on-being. The therapist's ability to handle the situation appropriately requires this understanding. If the therapist has problems in the power dimension, a countertransference resistance may be activated and a power struggle set in motion.

Perhaps experiencing relatively satisfactory caretaking only at times of illness as a very young child will lead to complaints of illness, real or not, as a way to capture the wished-for caretaking of the therapist. This strategy was a disguised attempt to gain power and control over the other. Once again, the therapist is likely to have unproductive countertransference reactions to the intensity and seeming intransigence of the patient's implicit, if not explicit, demands that he fix her. His own feelings of powerlessness may be stirred up. His cognitive capacity to stay clear about what is happening in the relationship should help him manage his own emotional responses to this difficult patient.

We also have to realize that the patient is not an infant, but an adult with mental resources the infant did not have. It is these resources that make treatment possible. Just as we must have empathy for the child he was, we must have respect for the adult he is now. The assessment of ego functions delineated in Chapter 1 will help the therapist feel on firmer ground about how to respond to these strategies. Will he function as an auxiliary ego, providing auxiliary sources of support for the patient, especially during absence or vacations, or will he be able to use careful interpretation? Still, the seriousness of the core problem should not be underestimated.

The primacy of the role of the mother in the evolution of the power dimension of human experience was articulated by a woman who told her therapist, "Mothers can make life okay in ways a father can't touch. Mothers can obliterate you. Fathers can't define you in such a fundamental way."

Attachment

The well-being of the child at this stage depends on the readiness of the primary caretaker to provide what Winnicott (1965) refers to as the "holding environment." He uses the term "holding" to denote "the total environmental provision." He calls the optimal attitude of the mother of the newborn "primary maternal preoccupation."

This picture of the baby before the twin processes of separation and individuation are under way may be reactivated in the very primitive patient or under conditions of regression. The patient will attempt to control the therapist so as to be able to use the therapist's power as if it were his own. He may use detachment as a defense against the dangers of overwhelming affect that might, once again, overtake him if he relies on what he perceives as an unreliable other or others. The detachment may be viewed as a character resistance. The attempts to control the therapist, to have power over him and his availability, will be seen as a transference resistance. This is another situation where an assessment of strengths as well as vulnerabilities is critical in the formulation of a treatment strategy.

It is during this stage of development that the child achieves what Erikson (1950) calls "basic trust," or basic distrust. The capacity for trust will be brought into the treatment relationship and will play a role in the setting up of a positive therapeutic alliance. A predominance of distrust will also be brought into the treatment relationship, bringing with it the potential for a paranoid, psychotic transference. If there is at least a modicum of trust established, even though it may be tentative, the outlook for therapeutic success is increased, although it will be a difficult situation. Trust of the power attributed to the therapist will be at issue. The quality of the child's experience during the attachment process will build certain characteristic feelings and expectations about the interpersonal world into the child's inner world. These feelings and expectations will include the child's sense of power or powerlessness in regard to the primary caretaker. In particular, it will have to do with the power of the baby to have an impact on the mother. His cries bring her attention. His needs evoke her response to those needs. When she responds, it is as if he now participates in her power. Without her intervention, he is totally powerless and helpless, a state that evokes overwhelming anxiety or overwhelming rage. Krystal (1978) writes about traumatic affect as affect that overwhelms the ego. It leads to a disorganization of the self.

The scenario of achieving power by sharing that of someone else who is perceived in an idealized manner, to whom both omnipotence and perfection are attributed, can become the template for all later power arrangements. Some women achieve a sense of power they do not feel in themselves through their attachment to a powerful man. The repetition of achieving a sense of power through participating in another's omnipotence and perfection, through attaching oneself to the powerful other, is a precarious strategy. The other probably will not fulfill those expectations. In the treatment situation, this is the set-up described by Kohut as the idealizing transference of the narcissistic personality disorder. The failure of the therapist to meet the patient's expectations—which are, in effect, demands—will set in motion the devaluing of the therapist and a retreat to the grandiose self. The thread of questions of power runs through these interactions. Who has it? Who does not? Will it be shared or will it be withheld? Will the individual have to regain his sense of power through the illusory grandiose self where he needs no one and is sufficient unto himself?

Furthermore, the other to whom all power is attributed may come to feel the burden of these expectations and may come to resent them. He or she may also fear the ready rage that will come his or her way from the dependent individual who feels disillusioned and disappointed. The patient may believe that the therapist has the power to give her what she wants or needs and is simply withholding it out of meanness or badness.

The therapist will be better able to manage these difficult transferences if she is aware of the power issues that are impacting her as well as the vulnerabilities behind the patient's need to have powerful control of her.

Moving Toward Separateness and Individuality

The beginnings of a conscious sense of intrinsic power emerge as the child gradually separates out from the interpersonal matrix of the mother–child dyad as a unique, individual self. Insofar as the primary caretakers support this process, the child will feel secure in being able to feel safely dependent on parental figures, and in being able to value and look up to the power attributed to them without envying or wanting to destroy it or steal it from them.

From about ten to sixteen months of life, the child's focus shifts increasingly to those "autonomous functions" that develop as a consequence of the maturation of the central nervous system—such as locomotion, perception, and the learning processes, including acquiring language and understanding concepts. The child is also increasingly confronted with the experience of its real separateness from mother. Her ready availability when she is needed and the pleasure the child derives from the mastery of new abilities make these small separations tolerable for the child. It is these new abilities that form the basis for a conscious awareness of intrinsic power. This includes the elation of being able to stand upright and, then, to walk alone. Mahler (1975) describes the time of this achievement as the peak point of the child's belief in his own magic omnipotence. But, she adds, it is still to a considerable degree derived "from his sense of sharing in his mother's magic powers" (20). Yet, the insistence on doing it himself, and the elation and pride that go with the mastery of small, yet monumental, tasks, are manifestations of the experience of intrinsic power. There is a growing consciousness of the "I am." Now it is joined with the "I can." Who cannot help but experience the child's joy with him when he exclaims, "I did it!"

When the parent's own needs lead her to interfere with the child's growing autonomy, she also interferes with the child's emerging intrinsic power. She has all the power. The child has none. It isn't hard to project this scenario into the treatment situation and the reenactment with the therapist. On one hand, the patient may submit to the therapist's abilities to think and know—which, of course, is a resistance to the process as well as a transference resistance. On the other hand, he may find ways to overthrow the therapist's power by denying the value of what she says or does. He renders the therapist impotent. The tables are turned and he is in the more powerful position with its associated pride, while the therapist is in the powerless position with its associated shame. These resistances must be addressed if the patient is to move past what could be an interminable impasse. "I've been noticing how quick you are to dismiss my comments out of hand. I know I could be wrong, but could there be something else going on?"

The potential for a countertransference acting-out—a countertransference resistance—is very high in such covert battles for power. The therapist has to have his own power issues well in hand so as not to play them out in the therapy situation.

Echoes of what Mahler names the "practicing period" and its magic omnipotence sometimes lead to persisting beliefs about the magical nature of one's innate abilities and powers. Learning to walk and talk do indeed come as if by magic, unlike the conscious effort one must make to learn the vocabulary of a foreign language. I have worked with some individuals who were clearly of superior intelligence and for whom learning had been effortless throughout their education. Paradoxically, they were far less secure about their abilities than people of lesser innate endowment. They didn't have the sense of conscious effort through the use of their own actual abilities, which gives one a feeling of some connection with and control over what one can and cannot do. One cannot rely on it. What comes magically can go away magically. These individuals are especially vulnerable to powerlessness and shame. They may develop a defensive, illusory sense of power that temporarily counteracts these unpleasant feelings, but illusion is unreliable and there is likely to be a chronic underlying anxiety. The person may be afraid to try something new that will require real effort. He will tell himself he is simply not interested in this activity when he is actually avoiding putting his omnipotence to the test. While the therapist may, in an unwise departure from neutrality, try to encourage him by supporting how capable he is, he will often simply rationalize his avoidance in terms of not valuing the goal in question. "I know I could get all A's, but I really don't care if I do or not. I don't want to waste my life studying all the time. It doesn't matter to me if I get into a good college or not." Options and future opportunities are foreclosed to this "underachiever." While this posture may have become characterological, the arguments with the therapist will be a manifestation of transference resistance, which must be confronted to dissolve the impasse. The power/powerlessness and pride/shame aspects of what looks like an ego-syntonic self-destruct mechanism must be elucidated along with the core relational problem.

From Babyhood to Childhood

As the child's sense of himself as a separate person rapidly advances, his parents are confronted with the fact that he is a person in his own right. Erikson (1950) speaks of the developmental task of the second year of life as the achievement of autonomy. The failure to do so leads to a sense of shame and doubt in the child. He notes how shaming a child "exploits an increasing sense of being small, which can develop only as the child stands up and as his awareness permits him to note the relative measures of size and power" (123). The first major thrust toward a change in the child's relationship to the power of his parents comes in the second year of life. It is here that the little boy or girl discovers the wonderful "no." The terrible two's are now in motion. Descartes wrote, "*Cogito, ergo sum.* I think, therefore I am." The two-year-old, asserting himself as a separate self, does so with the simple "no." "I say 'no,' therefore I am." Some of these children will have tantrums and insist on doing what they want to do, fighting the will of the parent. There are daily power struggles around the most minute aspects of interaction. The child may protest any act of initiative on the part of the mother. To the degree that the parents, who hold the ultimate power, are willing to share it *appropriately*, allowing for the necessary setting of limits and socialization, they reinforce the child's intrinsic power in a positive way. The patience of parents can be sorely tried and they may react angrily and punitively. The cost of asserting identity and will may be too high for the small child. On the other hand, out of some misdirected idea of what they feel they should do to support the child's initiative and autonomy, parents may submit to the child's tyranny. Unfortunately, instead of leading to self-confidence, this is more likely to generate anxiety-provoking beliefs of unrealistic power and an ability to overpower or destroy the parents on whom the child is really so dependent.

The major concern of the individual who presents himself to therapy with issues associated primarily with this stage of development is the loss of the support, love, and approval of the other. This was where he was derailed from the developmental continuum and the genesis of his core relationship problem. He may have come to believe, and still does, that assertion of his own will must lead to such loss. He may have developed a way of being with others based on submission or compliance, a state of chronic power-lessness and shame. This persisting dependent way of being with others shapes his adult relationships. While the other may be idealized at one level, at another he or she is also feared and envied because of the perceived power. He or she will be blamed when things do not go well.

This pattern is obviously one that will be brought into the relationship with the therapist and its acting out will be seen as transference resistance. Arising where it did in the second to third year of life, there will be many ego strengths on which the therapist can rely to do the analytic work.

CHILDHOOD AND COMPETENCE

It is interesting to note that the word "competence" stands midway between impotence and omnipotence. While the extremes are based on illusion or fantasy, the center (competence) is based on reality. Power issues that arise in childhood or adolescence are likely to be reprises of those from the earlier years and can be understood as an amalgam of issues from both times. Echoes from the separation–individuation phase will often be heard in adolescence where the conflict between the wishes to be taken care of and those to be independent will create a certain amount of turmoil in the boy or girl, as well as in his or her relationship with parents. Since similar defenses and adaptations with respect to power can arise at different stages of development, they will be associated with different core relationship problems and require different treatment strategies. As therapists, we must not jump to premature conclusions based on the presenting picture.

Erikson describes the childhood years as a time to develop "industry," a time to adjust oneself to the inorganic laws of the world of tools. Erikson says, "His ego boundaries include his tools and his skills. . . . [He learns] the pleasure of work completion by steady attention and persevering diligence" (227).

In power terms, childhood is a time to widen the experience of intrinsic power. Powers of the physical self develop through exertion of strength, speed, coordination, skill, and toleration of physical discomfort. These capacities are developed in competitive team sports such as baseball, softball, and soccer, along with the social capacity for team play. In the classroom, the intrinsic power of the intellect is similarly exercised. The ability to think becomes more and more complex, with the emergence of the capacity for abstract ideas. One six-year-old budding philosopher asked his mother, "How do we know that God is not dreaming us, and that when He wakes up is when we die?"

Erikson notes that if this inherent developmental thrust is inhibited because of preexisting unresolved conflicts within the family, the child will develop a sense of inferiority. At the same time, the core relationship problem will lead to a variety of strategies for coping with a failure to conquer the tasks of these years of childhood. These strategies will be brought into adult life and, in particular, into a relationship with a psychotherapist as transference resistance. Does the individual present with an attitude of meekness and deference from the very start?

In the competitive atmosphere of the classroom and the schoolyard, power takes on a different kind of significance. Power hierarchies develop along many lines and range from class leader to playground bully. The child's ability to be in this world without undue anxiety, without having to retreat in fear, or to develop a defensive "no one can push me around" attitude, will be affected in his relation to his own intrinsic power, as well as to the power of others or what he perceives as the power of others.

A child who envies the power of his parents may carry this same attitude toward teachers. When interpersonal struggles are enacted with teachers, overtly or covertly, the child may well be motivated to defeat the teacher. The interpersonal power struggle takes precedence over becoming knowledgeable and competent. Carried through to all major authority figures as the child gets older, eventually this struggle may be acted out in psychotherapy.

The child who competitively seeks to be best loved by the teacher and who sets up peers as either sibling or Oedipal rivals will be unable to explore new ways of competence in the peer world. Other children readily notice and react negatively to the attitude of superiority that comes to that child by virtue of being special to the powerful authority figure. They also react negatively to that child's obvious need to defeat them, to make them less-than. In group psychotherapy with adults, this dynamic is likely to be acted out once again. In one group, pointing out the theme of several members trying to be most special by being the sickest one—and thus needing more from the therapist—finally unblocked the group from its impasse. In individual psychotherapy, offhand comments about other patients, about others in the waiting room, or about the family the therapist is imagined to have will be important to bring forward for exploration. Often, they will be signs of the transference resistance embedded in these comments.

Children act out with their peers the needs they have for power and control. The playground bully turns the tables, trying to undo the shame and powerlessness of being bullied at home. Adults who get stuck on the power issues of the earlier years, and who were therefore unable to develop a real and valid sense of their own competence in childhood, often present themselves in therapy as "unable." This inability can refer to such matters as taking care of bills, managing personal business matters in general, or knowing what to do and how to do it in the adult world of travel and commerce. Intrinsic power has been foreclosed. There is a self-imposed impotence. This becomes a transference resistance, rendering the therapist equally power-less. He is blocked from having an effect.

The therapist has to ascertain the dynamic significance of this "inabil-ity." Did it evolve within an enmeshed family system in which the indi-vidual was assigned the role of the inept one or the dumb one? Did it become his "job" to be incompetent and thus enable the others in the fam-ily to feel superior? Or did he truly not develop the skills for living even though he is fully equipped intellectually to do so? Insisting on his own incompetence to the therapist and his need for the therapist to take over control of his life by endless advice-giving can be joined by a therapist with her own need to feel super competent and powerful. Countertrans-ference resistance will join transference resistance to generate, perhaps for years, this misalliance and collusion. The underlying dynamic and its sig-nificance in the core relationship problem won't be explored until the re-sistances to doing so are confronted.

Stierlin (1974) describes the ways in which adolescent individuation is blocked when "parents and children operate under the unspoken as-sumption that essential satisfactions and securities can be obtained only within the family. . . . [P]arents . . . see only one avenue open to them: to tie their children ever more closely to themselves" (36). This dynamic, which he refers to as "binding," starts in childhood before the heightened developmental thrust of adolescence comes into play with its stronger demand for autonomy and individuation. Stierlin describes three forms of binding. In *id binding*, exploitation of dependency needs is enabled by emphasis on regressive gratification. The adolescent is infantilized. *Ego binding* results as a consequence of the child's being made to feel doubtful and insecure about his own resources. The parent interferes with the child's differentiated self-awareness and self-determination through mys-tification and violation of cognitive integrity—undercutting the child's confidence in his ability to think. ("You say such stupid things! What is the matter with you!") *Superego binding* exploits loyalty. Guilt over wishes to break away is instilled. ("How can you do that to me?" "Don't you know you are killing your mother?") Children are turned into lifelong self-sacrificing victim-adjuncts to the family.

As adults, these individuals will be unwilling to give up the gratifica-tions of the infantile emotional goodies, or will be too frightened at the prospect of negotiating the world on their own. They may also feel too guilty at even the wish to separate. As a patient, these individuals may ex-perience the therapist as pushing them toward any one of these dangers. The importance of neutrality in this instance cannot be overemphasized. It may appear that progress in the treatment process is being made when we unexpectedly come up against the "negative therapeutic reaction," in which therapeutic success seems to make the person worse. The core relationship problem cannot be papered over with pseudo-achievement. There is a chronic power struggle as the therapist is doomed to fail by virtue of the transference resistance.

Freud described the negative therapeutic reaction in 1923, remarking that in the case of individuals who exhibit this reaction:

> There is no doubt that there is something . . . that sets itself against their recovery, and its approach is dreaded as though it were a danger. . . . [T]he need for illness has got the upper hand in them over the desire for recovery. If we analyse this resistance . . . even after allowance has been made for an attitude of defiance against the physician and for fixation to the various forms of gain from illness, the greater part of it is still left over; and this reveals itself as the most powerful of all obstacles to recovery. (Freud, [1923] 1961, 49)

It would be a mistake to assume that the only transference resistance is that of defiance, although there is indeed power in powerlessness. This assumption might, in some cases, activate a countertransference reaction of anger, believing the patient is just trying to defeat him or her in some kind of power dynamic, which, at an unconscious level, is true. But what is at issue is the core relationship problem in which this dynamic is embedded. The complexities of the core relationship problem will usually make this task equally complex. Perhaps the patient believes that the therapist, like mother or father, deep down does not want him to "get better," and that maintaining the unconscious connection to mother through the re-creation of this scenario protects him from the potential anxiety or depression of object loss. Understanding and working through the resistance *in terms of the core relationship problem* as it is played out with the therapist is the sine qua non for true improvement.

In the case of active family system pressures, we are not only dealing with past developmental derailments and conflicts and their residua; the conflicts are intense in the present. The cast of characters is still acting on the individual to render him unable to break away. *We cannot analyze the real.* If the parent is paying for the treatment, it is not likely to survive. The family's resistance becomes the patient's resistance to the therapy itself as well as to the therapist as an agent of the therapy. There is a dynamic triangle in which the patient feels caught between family and therapist. Family loyalty along with fear and guilt at damaging the family as an entity makes the regressive choice almost inevitable.

If we can engage the latent seeds of autonomy striving in the alliance, if the individual can get a job and pay for his own treatment, the prognosis is better. At that point, the conflicts can be brought into the treatment relationship where developmental derailment and the core relationship problems can be more successfully explored. Aside from the individual's participation in the pathological family dynamic, there is a split-off true self and the fear of relating from that state. Our task is to engage with this facet of the individual's personality and allow it to come into relationship with us. The defenses against the felt danger of allowing this to happen will be manifest in transference resistances, which must be carefully elucidated and explored. Power issues embedded in these resistances will become evident. The unblocking of intrinsic power—of the "I am," the "I can," and the "I will"—will be the desired outcome.

ADOLESCENCE AND ITS POWER DIMENSIONS

The boy's or girl's relationship to power—to the intrinsic power of the self versus a need for defensive or compensatory power; and to his or her characteristic role in the power balance within the family—will affect how he or she negotiates the developmental tasks of the teen years.

Assimilation of the new pubescent body, the physiological changes, and the upsurge of sexual desires as well as of testosterone-driven aggression in the boy, have to be achieved and then integrated into the sense of an ongoing self, the sense of "this is still me." Without the core solidarity of the intrinsic power of the *I am*, the new feelings can be fragmenting or disorganizing. Anxiety, uncertainty as to identity, and fear of losing control may be overwhelming. Eating obsessions often develop at this juncture, with an attempt to gain omnipotent control over the body, its form, and its impulses. This defensive illusion of power counteracts the terror of helplessness against forces over which one has no control. This new helplessness reevokes earlier terrors of helplessness and powerlessness against controlling and intrusive parents.

Another task is to establish the ability to relate to members of the opposite sex. In childhood, there was a tendency to group with members of the same sex, with the shared goals of developing skills and interests and a sense of one's self as a boy or as a girl through peer relating. Now the pull is in the other direction, to establish a sense of one's self as male or female through the eyes of the opposite sex, to have that maleness or femaleness affirmed through sexuality rather than through skills and interests.

Since boyfriends or girlfriends can take on the power to affirm the self, to make the self feel not only attractive but lovable, parental power may be attributed to such a friend. This makes the self especially vulnerable and open to feelings of powerlessness and shame once again. The more solid the sense of intrinsic power that developed in the earlier years, the less likely the young person is to suffer these agonies and to settle, once again, into a dependent and powerless position.

As an adult patient in psychotherapy, such a boy or girl may locate their unhappiness in their problems in adult love relationships. They may wish, overtly or covertly, that the therapist can tell them how to make these here-and-now relationships work. The therapist may be pulled into the role of counselor and advice-giver, once again putting the patient in the inferior position vis-à-vis the power of the authority figure. This would be another example of how a countertransference resistance can join with a transference resistance to generate an impasse in the treatment. Where a core relationship problem emerged that left this person in a state of powerlessness and shame vis-à-vis the powerful other will have to be uncovered. Exploring the dynamics of the transference–countertransference mix will shed light on this important issue.

Parents may have a strong need to maintain their power in the family power balance and keep their son or daughter in the more powerless and diminished position. In this situation, it may seem to the adolescent boy or girl that the only way to get the adult power that they increasingly feel is their due is to overthrow the authority of the parents. Even in healthy development, this to-be-expected shift in the relative power of the generations may bring a certain amount of discord. The terrible teens may remind parents of the terrible two's of their child's past. The developmental conflict between dependency and autonomy is present in both of these crisis points in psychological evolution. In effect, the parents of the adolescent have to be deposed; and if they feel shamed or diminished by this change in the balance of power, the young person will have to deal with the guilt of having somehow hurt the parents, or with the anxiety of feeling one has destroyed them and left oneself alone in the world.

Loewald (1979), in his paper "The Waning of the Oedipus Complex," writes that this involves facing and bearing guilt for two acts we consider criminal, even if these acts exist only in fantasy. The criminal acts he refers to are the incestuous fantasies of the Oedipus complex and what he views as a form of parricide: the murder of parental authority and the assumption of responsibility for one's own life that takes place with the severing of the emotional ties with parents. Incest is the "crime" associated with the Oedipal wishes, and parricide is the "crime" associated with the resolution of the Oedipus complex. "Not only parental authority is destroyed by wresting authority from the parents and taking it over, but the parents, if the process were thoroughly carried out, are being destroyed as libidinal objects as well" (757). He does note that if things go well, what will be left is tenderness, mutual trust, and respect—the signs of equality. Perhaps the intense energy and the heady new sense of power of the older adolescent has something to do with the power this age group arrogates unto itself in many countries and societies. It is their turn to run the world!

Once the psychotherapist has alerted himself or herself to the potential for power issues to run through the therapist–patient relationship, he or she will discover that there are many variations in the theme in addition to those touched on in this chapter. The therapy relationship is a microcosm, a special laboratory in which the patient can experience, confront, overcome, transform, or transcend the barriers to satisfying love and work. These barriers often relate to power issues, and the therapy situation offers an opportunity for the individual to confront these rather than continuously act them out in inevitably self-defeating behaviors.

Envy and spoiling that which is envied is often associated with issues of power. When it is the therapist who is envied, a transference resistance will come into play. The next chapter explores this scenario.

7

✿

Envy as Resistance

Almost four hundred years ago Sir Francis Bacon (qtd. in Evans 1968) wrote in his essay "On Envy" that "envy is ever joined with the comparison of a man's self; and where there is no comparison, no envy." As an all-consuming passion, it was well described around twenty-four hundred years ago by the Greek philosopher Antisthenes (qtd. in Evans 1968) with the analogy: "As iron is eaten by rust, so are the envious consumed by envy." Today psychoanalysts have observed that envy is "an exquisitely irrational phenomenon, insofar as it pursues no other serviceable end than that of attacking what is valuable in the other, including his capacity of giving it to us" (Etchegoyen et al. 1987). Thus envy generates an ever-increasing sense of frustration and deprivation, which is in large part self-imposed; it often gets in the way of receiving from others what might actually be available.

Etchegoyen et al. point out that envy ultimately *must* spoil what is good. The person who may have been seen as good automatically becomes bad because of the very fact that he or she evokes envy. Thus, what is good is made bad, and what is bad and thus not to be envied becomes paradoxically good. Clearly this relates to the patient and his therapist. One man said to me in a session, "I contrast myself with what I think you have, all the things I'd like to achieve. It stops me from taking you as a model, from taking in the positive aspects, because if I take from you I have to acknowledge what you possess and that only increases the envy."

Another patient came into one session reporting that she had wanted to tear up some scientific magazines I had in the waiting room, in a fury that

I could understand them and she could not. Exploration of the major issue of envy and envious rage revealed that not only did she envy those she saw as powerful, but she also feared their envy if they knew of her grandiosity and contempt. While envy evokes hatred of the one who is envied, the fear of being envied leads to self-sabotage so as not to be perceived by the other as enviable. She does not want her projected hatred coming back at her. Both halves of this dynamic will be activated vis-à-vis the therapist as a transference resistance. The dynamic leads to an impasse in her life and in her therapy as well.

In the spirit of envy, one might be moved to trash what the other has of value. Then it can be rejected as not worthy of being envied. This dynamic is referred to as "spoiling." While the patient needs the therapist to be strong and to have the power to help him or her, the patient may envy and hate that power as well. Thus, envy is the source of a transference resistance.

A woman who characteristically clung to a powerless position to force her mother to take care of her, as well as to protect her mother against the hate of her own envy of the older woman's power, said of an associate, "I hate her, and there's nothing that can be done about it. I spoil her by thinking that her seams are crooked, or that she only *seems* nice because she is so shallow. I'm powerless with her. I do want to smash her, to get rid of her, to tell her what I think of her. And I hate *you* [the therapist] for being so strong. I feel impotent. I can't change you. I'll kiss ass and walk away hating you. It's a passive ragefulness."

Although this patient used to think of herself as competitive, she came to understand the critical difference between competitiveness and envy. This difference resides in the degree of hostility and the wish to spoil or destroy that go with envy. One can value the competitive rival and have no wish to harm that person. In competitiveness, unlike envy, the only wish is to win.

ENVY AND TABOO

Envy and admiration are similar insofar as they both entail a "looking-up-to" attitude toward the other. The more attainable the admired qualities of achievements, the more the other stands as a model for one's own development. A major distinction between envy and admiration is the element of taboo. We can emulate what we admire. We can aspire to it and pursue it. There are no barriers beyond our own ability to achieve the goal. In the case of envy, however, there is usually an unwritten and unspoken law. Not only do you not have it—you *may not* have it. It is not permitted to you no matter what your ability to achieve it. In his *Essay on*

Man, Alexander Pope (Evans 1968) wrote: "Envy, to which th' ignoble mind's a slave./Is emulation in the learn'd or brave."

Racker (1957) noted that the prerequisite to envy is a painful recognition that one lacks what the other has. In my view, the added dictum "and you have no right to it" is the sine qua non for setting up the envy dynamic, rather than such recognition as evoking a determination to get it for oneself. In run-of-the-mill competition, there is no need to destroy or devalue what the other has and no barrier to the person going after it for himself or herself.

Freud ([1916] 1957) describes some people as "wrecked by success." He comments on how bewildering it is to find that "people occasionally fall ill precisely when a deeply-rooted and long-cherished wish has come to fulfillment. It seems then as though they were not able to tolerate happiness" (316). Freud was bound by his assumption that it is frustration that induces illness. He did note that external frustration is not per se pathogenic. It is the frustration that results from internal conflict that is the problem. He writes further that "analytic work has no difficulty in showing us that it is forces of conscience which forbid the subject to gain the long hoped-for advantage from the fortunate change in reality. It is a difficult task, however, to discover the essence and origin of these judging and punishing trends" (318).

Freud's discussion of the literary characters created by Shakespeare and Ibsen led him to conclude that "psycho-analytic work teaches us that the forces of conscience which induce illness in consequence of success, instead of, as normally, in consequence of frustration, are closely connected with the Oedipus complex, the relation to father and mother—as perhaps, indeed, is our sense of guilt in general" (331). It seems that although Freud understood the interpersonal origins of the Oedipus complex, once he saw things in terms of his structural paradigm, in terms of conscience—that is, superego—and guilt, he abandoned the relational implications of the unresolved conflict in the here and now. In my view, whether fear is a fear of someone's jealousy or envy or the fear of losing someone's love, it is a relationship problem that continues to affect the individual's way of being in the world, and it often stands in the way of the individual's ability to achieve or tolerate success.

Melanie Klein (1975) sees envy as contributing to the "infant's difficulties in building up his good object, for he feels that the gratification of which he was deprived has been kept for itself by the breast that frustrated him." She emphasizes that "envy is the angry feeling that another person possesses and enjoys something desirable—the envious impulse being to take it away or to spoil it" (180–81).

I disagree with Klein insofar as she sees this situation going back to the beginning of life. The dynamic of envy requires a level of cognitive development not yet achieved by the infant. The infant in the situation described by Klein will be tossed back and forth between extreme pleasure and extreme displeasure or rage. If this situation is chronic and interferes with the organization of a cohesive self and the sense of going-on-being, pathology of structure will be the outcome. In my view, the dynamic of envy will emerge with the cognitive achievement and conscious awareness of a powerless self that is compared to the all-powerful parent.

ENVY AND DEVELOPMENTAL DERAILMENT

As in most situations, the time of psychological derailment from the developmental continuum cannot be assumed from the presenting or later emerging problem alone—that of envy in this discussion. As noted above in the discussion of Klein's view of envy, the derailment may be at the most primitive level, leading to a pathological organization of self- and object representations. The resistances encountered will be in the service of protecting the self from dissolution, from object loss and the anaclitic depression, or from paranoid terrors. Envy of the therapist and its role in transference resistance will certainly complicate the treatment of such a patient. Whether or not it can be confronted and explored by the therapist will be decided on a case-to-case basis, depending on the relative strengths and weaknesses of the ego. In my view, the envy, per se, would have emerged later when the child was further along in cognitive development and able to think about his feelings in words. He is not only subject to emotional turmoil at the moment of the unpleasant interaction with the powerful other. He also dwells on it in his mind. He thinks about it and often elaborates on it. A patient may describe this as "stewing" about something.

In perhaps the majority of cases in which envy emerges in the clinical material or in a transference resistance, the point of derailment would have been at the point of the rapprochement crisis. As discussed in chapter 1, the rapprochement phase marks the final step in separation and individuation.

At around the age of eighteen months, the toddler becomes increasingly aware of his or her separateness from mother and mother's separateness from him or her. Language begins to play an increasing role in interaction and in the child's attempts to make sense of his experience. Beliefs about the self, about the other, and about interpersonal relationships are now being established in words. These beliefs, of course, are distorted because of cognitive limitations. Yet, they may persist unchanged and become the basic premise for all future reasoning about that person's interpersonal experiences, good or bad (Horner 1997).

At this point in development, there is a conscious awareness of the need for the other who is now perceived as powerful. The child is confronted with his or her relative powerlessness. If the primary caretaker uses power in a benign and helpful manner, that power is the basis for the child's sense of security. If, on the other hand, parental power is experienced as against the self, as something that is not only given but is also withheld, the child comes to both envy and hate that power and will develop techniques to control it. The envy will have its own dynamic in interfering with the establishment of positive and healthy interpersonal relationships. Issues of power and envy are often intertwined. It will be important for the therapist to tease these two threads apart so they may be elucidated and interpreted historically and in the transference resistance as well.

CHILDHOOD: ENVY IN THE FAMILY SYSTEM

In childhood, past the stage of separation and individuation, other sources of envy arise. In some families, different attributes are assigned to the different family members: Susan is the "pretty one." Marion is the "reliable one." George is the "smart one." Francis is the "talented one." Even though there may be some basis for seeing differences between the children, when those differences become too important, they take on the property of *defining* that child—and also, by implication, defining the others in terms of *what they are not.* "No point in being reliable if that asset belongs to Marion." "I won't try to be pretty. Susan is the pretty one." "No point in thinking about college; George is the smart one." Assets assigned to someone else and not acknowledged as true of oneself as well will beget envy of that quality and the belief that it is *taboo to one's self.* Family unity and survival is perceived as requiring this composite identity. Changes in any of its separate elements are feared as destructive to family unity or as destructive to the most important members of the family—one or both parents. This kind of system is often referred to as an "enmeshed" family.

To the extent that a person disowns his or her own strengths, assets, and abilities—abilities that he or she does indeed have—in order to prevent the dreaded family disintegration, he or she will envy and hate others who seemingly have permission to claim them. This will apply to the therapist as well. Perhaps only the therapist has the right to insight, or intuition, or theoretical information. The patient will present as stupid or unknowledgeable when he is not. In many such situations, this will prove to be a highly educated and even professionally highly achieving man or woman. If the therapist does not recognize and confront this transference resistance, putting it into its historical and family context as well, the patient will never change. He or she will have to stay "dumb." These therapies often end unsatisfactorily and the patient will go on to another therapist—perhaps to a succession of therapists—with the same transference resistance, creating the same impasse.

After not too long, the therapist may catch herself answering the patient's questions, the answers to which there can be no doubt the patient already knows. A countertransference resistance, a collusion with the patient's transference resistance, can all too easily be set in motion in these situations. Together, they have been playing out the family rule. Once the therapist becomes aware of what is going on, she must point this out, including her own unconscious participation. Elucidation of the family system in which the patient is still enmeshed as well as its joint anxieties and defenses will be part of the interpretation. Depending on the degree to which the patient is still financially dependent on the parents, the difficulty in resolving his dilemma will be greater or lesser. The tighter the system, the more likely there will be family pressures on the patient to leave treatment. The therapist will have become the enemy of the family. It may sometimes be possible to head this off if the patient is financially self-sufficient, and if his situation is one from which he consciously, if not unconsciously, wants to escape.

Calogeras and Alston (1985) write about the relationship between family pathology and the infantile neurosis. They describe the situation in which the pathological family milieu succeeds in providing a certain *critical state* for the maintenance of the childhood in adulthood, and how it is a major inhibiting force in the failure to resolve the pathology. It is important for the therapist who works with the psychoanalytic model to understand the developmental implications of the pathological family system, and to understand that what we see clinically at times is the patient's *adaptation to that system*, an adaptation that has pathological sequelae. To interpret the sequelae from the point of view of the individual's psychology apart from that system will constitute a serious failure to understand her. Her internal world will contain the complexities and paradoxes of the pathological family system. Until these issues are confronted in therapy, the person will remain hostage to the system no matter how much work is done from the perspective of individual development. It will be important for the therapist to point out that there is, in effect, a triangle between herself, the patient, and the patient's family, and how both of them are caught in it.

The dynamics of the pathological family system will inevitably capture the developing child, usually at that point at which she has emerged out of the total dependency of infancy and begins to take on the unique characteristics of the young child. These characteristics, more or less, determine what is projected onto the child and what role is assigned to her. The child is also developing language at this time, enabling the verbal communication that also becomes a major vehicle for shaping the child into her role. There may have been relatively healthy development before this switch point. The strengths that come from a good beginning will be manifest in the patient as an adult. The point of derailment and capture by the family system is more likely to occur as the child moves into the individuation of early childhood. The transference resistance will relate specifically to the patient's role in the family system. The core relationship problem will be one of conflicted individuation and expression of one's own identity or will.

If the family pathology didn't allow for good-enough care in infancy and toddlerhood, character resistances may also come into play when the patient senses a danger to his sense of self-cohesion. With this patient, the therapist will have to be especially tuned in to where the individual is on the "empathy-anxiety gradient" (see Bromberg 1980, 22) at any given moment. Is he at the earlier level of structural impairment or at the later level of family irrational role assignment?

THE FAMILY ROLE AND INTERMINABLE TREATMENT

From Freud ([1937] 1964) on, the problem of interminable treatment has been considered from a variety of theoretical perspectives. In his analysis of a young Russian man, Freud writes: "We advanced no further in clearing up the neurosis of his childhood, on which his later illness was based, and it was obvious that the patient found his present position highly comfortable and had no wish to take any step forward which would bring him nearer to the end of his treatment" (217). Freud attempted to understand interminable analysis within the limits of his theory of the time, writing that "a constitutional strength of instinct and an unfavorable alteration of the ego acquired in its defensive struggle...are the factors which are prejudicial to the effectiveness of analysis and which make its duration interminable" (221).

While there may be a variety of core relationship problems and their associated resistances leading to this impasse, the one we are considering here is that of the taboo on certain ego strengths that come out of the enmeshed family system and its assignment of roles, which are both definitive and exclusionary of who each person is. It is the power of the taboo in shaping his life that leads to a sometimes virulent envy of those who do not labor under such restrictions in their lives. And, of course, when one of these is the therapist, envy and the fear of being envied will form the nexus of the transference resistance. Unless it is dealt with, the impasse can go on for years.

The next chapter demonstrates that the therapist's collusion with a compensatory identification that defends against the shame of childhood often leads to a pseudo cure. The transference resistance also protects the patient from that shame.

8

The "Constructed Self"
As Resistance

THE CONSTRUCTED SELF

In his paper, *Language and Psychoanalysis,* Richardson (1987) describes the horrendous history of a patient named Norma Jean Baker and the creation of Marilyn Monroe. Well before that time, Norma Jean had started to construct an identity that would bring her a sense of worth and pride. It also brought her a sense of safety, based on her fantasies of being rescued by an idealized father and later based on her immersion in the world of film and its stars. Her inquiry, laughingly made to an autograph-seeker, "How do you spell Marilyn Monroe?" was a clear statement of the split between her real and constructed selves.

The constructed self (Horner 1988) is not a false self in the Winnicott (1965) sense. The false self is basically a relational self and it is shaped in accord with the unconscious needs and projections of the primary care-takers. When the mother's intercessions are impingements—intrusions into or disruptions of the spontaneous experiencing of the child—its own self-directed flow of attention and movement becomes reactive instead. When this situation is chronic, rather than the occasional failure of the mother to be "good-enough," identity becomes consolidated around the reactions vis-à-vis the impinging other. Identity may also become consolidated around parental projections of some rejected and projected aspects of themselves. The false self-identity, which *feels* real, serves two functions. It enables and maintains a connection to the parent, and protects the hidden true self from them. It is because of its critical function of object-connecting that it is so difficult to give up in treatment.

81

Winnicott writes: "A principle might be enunciated, that in the False Self area of our analytic practice we find we make more headway by recognition of the patient's nonexistence than by a long-continued working with the patient on the basis of ego-defense mechanisms" (152). The constructed self, on the other hand, evolves as a defense against intolerable shame and self-hatred. It is shaped in accord with a fantasy ego-ideal. It is not grandiose in the usual sense of the term, but it must be perfect in order to maintain it, lest the shame erupt once again in full force. This defensive strategy is conscious and deliberate. The shame-ridden self is not repressed. It is hidden.

There will be multiple resistances in play. Relating to the therapist through the constructed self will constitute a transference resistance. Resistance to the work itself will serve to protect the individual from the eruption of shame. Failure to understand the patient's structure and dynamics may result in a countertransference resistance. The therapist may engage the constructed self in the alliance and participate in the patient's conscious agenda of making the constructed self more perfect. The patient earnestly asks for help in here-and-now life difficulties, inviting a nonanalytic counseling stance on the part of the therapist. Depending on the quality of early development and the presence of early derailment, there may be character resistances as well, by means of which a fragile self-cohesion will be protected. The conscious and deliberate creation of a constructed self requires the cognitive capacities of the somewhat older child or the adolescent. Yet, it is critical to understand the underlying character structure. Where was this person derailed from the developmental continuum, and what is the resulting core relationship problem? How did this issue make the child or teenaged boy or girl susceptible to such unbearable shame that creation of the constructed self was the only way out? Good-enough parenting that enables the child to develop a healthy and realistic self-esteem, as well as a firm sense of intrinsic power, may not make the boy or girl less unhappy with difficult life circumstances. This unhappiness, however, will not make it necessary to deny identifications with the parents and, thus, with one's own self.

Unfortunately, it is easy to collude with the patient in his or her earnest attempts at improvement and better functioning of the constructed self. The therapist will have been co-opted into setting up the therapeutic alliance with a wished-for fantasy identity.

INTERPRETATION OF THE SPLIT

The most important interpretation with respect to the constructed self is its defensive function. In this work, I will generally point out that it is as though there was a sheet of glass laid over the original self, with the new self constructed on top of the glass. Unlike the situation of dissociated self-states, each is fully conscious of the other. Although each can see the other, there can be no communication between them. The real self cannot avail itself of the achievements and positive feedback that comes to the constructed self in order to evolve a healthy and realistic self-esteem. The constructed self, on the other hand, cannot avail itself of the sense of authenticity that is attached to the rejected real self. There is a refusal to acknowledge any identification with the real self. There is a violent and complete split between the self who is and the self the person wants to be. Once again, it should be noted that the process is deliberate and conscious. This mechanism is often found in women with a history of sexual molestation in childhood. In these situations, the intensity of the combined shame and guilt motivated the defense.

One woman in her early forties had been molested by both grandfathers from the age of three until she stopped them both when she turned twelve. She recalled how the grandfather she really loved told her if she told anyone, her father would kill him and then the father would be sent to prison. Needless to say, she never told. She reported how she had decided at a very young age to be a movie star, and in fact, had a few minor roles in several films. We can see in her early choice of career a wish to flee from who she really was through pretending to be someone else as an actress. She developed problems that led her to seek therapy when she began to take lessons in method acting. This technique requires the individual to reach into the deepest recesses of the unconscious to access the range of affect required by the role the person is to play. This sent her into such a panic she was never able to act again.

The woman had had a variety of unsuccessful treatments, and I was to join the list of failed therapists. I brought up the issue of the constructed self and how I was often drawn into colluding with her to perfect it. In fact, she did not experience those sessions as helpful. This collusion, of course, demonstrated the joining of her resistance with that of the therapist. She felt good about sessions when she got to the buried feelings and cried. Then she would be upset at how the crying affected her appearance, and did not want to pursue this way of working. It jeopardized the perfection of the constructed self. She was a beautiful woman with a lovely and seductive quality of a young girl.

Early in her treatment, she invited me to a large Hollywood party she was giving, telling me it would help me build my practice. I thanked her for the invitation, but explained how I would become another in a list of people who exploited her for their own needs if I were to accept. She was not especially pleased at my response as she clearly wanted to co-opt me and her treatment into her constructed life. There was a resistance to a dependent transference, which would bring her in touch with who she was as a child. She hoped she could have a pseudo therapy in her pseudo identity. There are certainly a number of therapists who rationalize their joining in this kind of misalliance out of their own countertransference resistance to doing the hard work and dealing with the split-off self, and to giving up the narcissistic gratification offered them.

Finally, she left treatment when she was about to marry a very wealthy man who would enable her to live the life of one of the "beautiful people" (her words). When the defensive constructed self works, there is little or no motivation for analysis.

Dr. Richardson noted how Marilyn Monroe's analyst would take her home to visit with his family, possibly with the hope of providing corrective family and home experiences. But it was not Norma Jean who visited with his family. It was Marilyn Monroe. Their excitement at having Marilyn Monroe as a guest at their home co-opted her therapist into her constructed life.

As the constructed self is often the most attractive in a variety of ways, the therapist must resist the gratifications that accompany participation in it. If the therapist acts out this way, the patient is very likely to get the message that the therapist prefers the constructed self to the split-off shame- and guilt-ridden identity. Hereafter, her resistance to working with the split-off self will be intensified.

There are similar developmental discontinuities when an individual immigrates to a new country where a different language is spoken. Affect is likely to be contained in the mother tongue. There is good reason to believe that treatment will be facilitated if the therapist can speak the patient's original language. A constructed self may have been created with the individual's disidentifying with his or her own past. Sometimes American-born children of immigrants are embarrassed by the demeanor and foreign accent of their parents and are driven to achievement as a way to disidentify with the parents.

Another woman's constructed self entailed ridding herself of her New York accent. Her polished speech tended to be hesitant, her words measured. With the interpretation of the defensive function of the constructed self and the exploration of the childhood traumas endured as her real child self, she began to feel free to let the old language patterns come out. There was a release of affect and spontaneity as well.

THE WRONG SIDE OF THE TRACKS

Children want to be proud of their parents, of their family, and of their home. As they get older and meet children from very different circumstances than theirs, they may feel embarrassed at the comparison, that their house isn't as nice, their car old and dented, their clothes hand-me-downs. When mother feels ashamed because father can't keep a job, that shame permeates the atmosphere and is picked up by the children. The mother who feels ashamed because the father abandoned the family passes that shame on to the children as well. Now they are all "second-class citizens." The degree to which externals become a matter of deep shame depends on family relationships and parental attitudes. Living up to standards and values not based on material wealth can nourish pride in family and self. When the child's formative years are spent in an atmosphere of unhappiness and shaming, growing up on the wrong side of the tracks can come to be a stigma that must be erased. The shame of what is on the outside matches the shame felt on the inside. Materialistic values coupled with deprived life circumstances are likely to lead to shame. Money and success come to be linked to pride, if not actual superiority over those less fortunate.

Such a child may spend the rest of his life trying to be outstanding, accomplished, or rich enough to counteract the shame. A constructed self as a wealthy, successful businessman or professional person takes on a defensive value, helping him hide the person he grew up being from others and from himself. Sometimes, those trying to live a better life through a constructed self not only change their names, but also, through extensive surgery, their appearances. A greater and greater separation takes place between the early-formed, shame-ridden identity and the pride-based identity this person keeps trying to perfect. But the public identity the person has worked so hard to construct feels fundamentally and increasingly fraudulent. He or she is always afraid the truth will be found out. One can take the boy out of shantytown, but one cannot take shantytown out of the boy! The dividing sheet of glass is carefully kept intact.

ATTENDING TO THE PROCESS AND THE TRANSFERENCE–COUNTERTRANSFERENCE MIX

Because of the inevitable unhappiness and anxieties associated with this strategy, people with constructed selves often find their way to therapy. Complaining that their lives are not working for them, they want help in making the constructed self more perfect, and do not care to deal with the rejected, hated self. No matter how sensitively the therapist tries to address the shame of the early years and family relationships, the patient is likely to get angry at the therapist who tries to expose her secret self, and so may end the treatment. She only wants the therapist to focus on her constructed self and tries to control him so that he will do so. However she does this, the transference resistance will have to be attended to by the therapist. Getting caught up in the content may obscure what is going on in the process. Perhaps the individual is secretly comparing his hidden self with the therapist, assuming the therapist will look down on him if he exposes what is hidden. Perhaps the patient will experience the therapist as trying to force him to acknowledge his shame and, thus, shame him again.

The therapist has to take into consideration the patient's vulnerabilities, with due respect for his or her feelings of safety and self-esteem, particularly when there is significant structural pathology of the split-off real self. In these instances, the transference resistance may lie on top of a character resistance that is protecting a fragile, real self. The significance of the developmental history, the assessment of the point of derailment from the developmental continuum, and the core relationship problem can be forgotten more readily when the therapeutic alliance appears to be one with a constructed self. Despite the patient's resistance to dealing with his past, the therapist must keep his understanding of it in mind as an organizing principle of what is going on in treatment.

When a child is subjected to the distortions of reality resulting from the mental and behavioral problems of the parents, he is mystified about the world and people. Not having a degree in psychoanalysis, he can only come up with conclusions possible on the basis of his limited understanding of his world. Myths grow where knowledge cannot. The next chapter shows how some common myths of childhood come to the fore in psychotherapy.

9

The Need to Understand
as Resistance

In his book *The Developing Mind: Toward a Neurobiology of Interpersonal Experience*, Daniel Siegel (1999) explains how the mind emerges from the activity of the brain. He shows how this development is directly shaped by early childhood relationships. Siegel points out that the primary ingredient of a child's emotional security is the pattern of emotional communication between the child and his or her primary caretaker. As human beings, we cannot be understood solely in terms of biological and neurological health or disease.

The innocence and naiveté of young children can be funny and endearing. Meredith's father was a bank vice president. He had tried to explain to his children that he went to work every day to make money. Meredith was overheard explaining to her friend how her daddy made ten-dollar bills at the bank where he worked. She didn't have a clue as to what her father actually meant by "making money."

UNDERSTANDING THE MIND OF THE OTHER

Young children are mystified about what makes the world work and about what makes people tick, so to speak. As Siegel reports, child development researchers have found that the child's emerging understanding of the minds of others develops out of the earliest interactions between parents and child. Children only gradually come to have an understanding of how mental states are behind all action, including their own. As we know, the "understanding" may be seriously skewed when the relationship between the child and her parents is a troubled one. It will be especially distorted when the mind of the parent is driven by the irrationalities of her unconscious. In normal development, mystification gives way to understanding when the world presented to the child lends itself to logical, albeit often mistaken, interpretation.

Researchers Mayes and Cohen (1996) explore how and when children understand and act on knowledge that their parents have mental states that guide *their* actions toward their children and others. The individuation process moves the child toward an increasing awareness of the separateness of himself from his mother. This includes the separateness of their minds. Blocking of individuation may also block this cognitive achievement. Mayes and Cohen look at the gradual emergence of the child's ability to attribute to others the thoughts, beliefs, feelings, or desires that differ from their own. Clearly, this achievement will frequently lead to interpersonal conflict between parents and child. When this conflict is overly disturbing to the child, he or she may retreat to a denial of their separateness and seek the security of mental twinship. When this is a point of derailment from the developmental continuum, the resulting core relationship problem will be met as a source of resistance in psychotherapy. Kohut (1971) refers to the twinship transference as the most primitive of the narcissistic transferences met in the clinical situation. The patient assumes she and the therapist are alike in all ways, including how their mind works. The critical connection with the other is maintained at the cost of the existential separateness of the self. While this false belief creates a character resistance in the treatment, the fragility of the patient's character structure precludes premature confrontation, lest it cause the dissolution of the self.

Mayes and Cohen cite the long-recognized observation that children growing up in chaotic, inconsistent homes marred by violence and neglect are indiscriminate and unpredictable in how they relate to others. They are unable to anticipate familiar scenes or to tolerate the unexpected. The images of others are poorly developed, fragmented, or inconsistent. Such unfortunate beginnings limit the child's ability to understand the mind of the other. This limitation leads to anxiety, confusion, and mystification about the nature of human reality and what governs the actions of others. In an environment characterized by mystification, the child will try to explain to himself what is going on around him and inside him. He may come up with a myth that alleviates the mystification and offers some, albeit false, sense of predictability and control.

MYSTIFICATION AND THE MYTHICAL "IT"

The amorphous, undefined, magical "it" is constructed by a child trying to connect what he does, feels, says, or even just wishes to how his parents relate to him. At the same time, he undergoes a great deal of difficulty with this developmental task. He may think to himself, "She's angry because I did something to make her angry, but I don't know what that was." He is frightened because there is no way to figure out how to behave so that his mother will not be angry at him any more. He grows up thinking if he can just "do it right," he will be safe in his relationships. However, he will be puzzled as to what the "it" is. He is likely to extend this to his therapist, at which time the mythical "it" becomes the basis for a transference resistance. He will try to figure the therapist out so as to prevent anything bad from happening between them.

In the happier situation of relatively healthy and mature parents, the child will be able to learn the logical and consistent connection between his actions and the reactions of his parents. He may think, "When I'm helpful, Mommy really appreciates me and smiles at me. If I'm happy about something, she is glad for me and she is happy too. If I'm disobedient, I know she will get angry. If I say bad words, I know I'll get sent to my room. If I'm mean to someone, she'll want me to apologize."

The gradual internalization of parental approvals and disapprovals leads to the build-up of conscience, values, and standards of right and wrong. In the process of socialization, the child also learns within the culture of the family about what kinds of behaviors are acceptable in the wider culture. In addition, he learns whether or not parents are, for the most part, "in sync" with that wider culture. Conflict often arises within the child and between him and his parents, especially in immigrant families whose old ways are very different from what the child comes to experience in the world at large. "That's not how we do it" comes up against "but that's how everyone else does it."

Whether the parents are on the strict end of the continuum or on the more lenient end is less an issue with respect to mystification than is their clarity and predictability. There is considerable room for difference within the healthy spectrum of human behavior. Problems arise, however, when parental behaviors and attitudes toward the child are determined by the idiosyncratic nature of *their* psychology. They may be envious of the child's talents, or they may even hate a particular one of their children because of her resemblance to the grandmother whom the mother hates. Father may fly into rages stirred up under the influence of alcohol. In the presence of these or any other unfathomable and mystifying factor, the child will still try to explain to himself his parent's behavior as being a reaction to who he, the child, is and what he does. Piaget (1952) refers to the "egocentric" reasoning of the very young child. He comes to believe in the mythical it. "If I did *it* right, she wouldn't have taken drugs." "If I do *it* right, she will love me." Later in life this may become "If I do *it* right, I can get a man."

This kind of mystification of the young child leads to a derailment from the developmental continuum, leading to a denial of separateness.

Cognitive clarity is essential to a healthy negotiation of the developmental continuum. The core relationship problem becomes consolidated around the mythical it. The desperate attempt to define the "it" and put it into action is part of the illusion that one has complete control over the other, starting with mother. Somehow the child believes how good or bad he is, how loving or rejecting he is, how mean or kind he is, will determine what mother is like at that moment. The fact that her mother may have a headache, be worried about money, or be upset at her own mother would never enter the child's mind. There is an illusion of total power over the parent, despite the fact that the child feels so powerless. There is a denial of separateness between the self and the other. Acknowledgment of that separateness would destroy any hope the child may cling to for making the relationship with the desperately needed mother better by doing "it" right. If the child loses hope, he feels the despair that goes with hopelessness. But sadly, it is a false hope.

The Mythical "It" as a Resistance

In psychotherapy, this situation will create a complex of resistances. The transference resistance will be a re-creation of having to figure out what the mythical "it" is in order to protect the good relationship with the therapist. A resistance to the work of uncovering the role of the mythical "it" and the consequences of letting go of the hope of being able to control the object will protect the patient from experiencing the painful loss of the "potential good mother" and the depression that goes with object loss. She is a "potential" because she exists only in the mind of the child who wishes and hopes he can bring her into reality by "doing it right." The confronting of manifestations of the myth whenever they appear and the elucidation of the dynamic and the anxiety behind it are necessary to loosen the hold they have on the patient. An empathic understanding of his need to preserve hope when he was a child and of the pain of letting go of the false hope now will support the patient in the very painful work in this area.

In adult life, the "it" may take on a definite shape, such as "I can't be too successful or mother will envy and hate me." Then life will be directed by this belief, with self-sabotage as the road to earning mother's care and love. This may lead to smoldering resentment behind a false front of inadequacy or failure. However, when the "it" continues to be indefinable, the individual lives with inordinate anxiety about doing the "wrong" thing. That person feels unable to figure out a safe way to be in the world, afraid to make choices or decisions or to act on them once they are made. The individual may become immobilized and relationships will be avoided because they stir up so much anxiety about "doing it wrong."

In therapy, this kind of anxiety may result in a resistance to a dependent transference. The patient will not want to risk allowing the therapist to have too much power in the relationship. The ability of the therapist to discern the role of the mythical it, its origins, its functions, and its costs, as well as to empathically comment on how much fear the person brings into the room, will be essential to dissolving the impasse that exists from the start. The core relationship problem as it is acted out in the therapy relationship will be the organizing principle of the work. In most such cases, this problem arose at the rapprochement stage of the developmental continuum. With the development of language came the ability to consciously "think about" something. But in continuing to deny their separateness, the individual clings to the illusion of the power to control the other. However, there will be a cohesive self and the ego-strength on which one can rely. The individual will be able to withstand the confrontation of his distortion of reality and participate in the working alliance.

The next chapter considers several generalized attitudes about one's self and about the world, which may surface as resistances in psychotherapy. They become rationalizations behind which the patient hides.

10

Common Attitudes as Sources of Resistance

An attitude is defined as "a state of mind or feeling with regard to some matter; disposition." Disposition is defined as "one's customary manner of emotional response." It is a *habitual frame of mind.* This frame of mind is set in place in reaction to early relationship conflicts. They have come to be one's customary manner of emotional response. When someone says, "I don't like your attitude," he may be responding to several subtle indicators of your emotional state of mind. These may be one's facial expression, one's tone of voice, the words one uses, or one's body language.

If we keep in mind that our patient's attitudes have come out of an early relationship conflict, exploring those attitudes may begin to peel away the defenses against dealing with the core relationship conflict. Furthermore, the therapist can be alert to subtle or not-so-subtle manifestations of these attitudes toward him or her—in other words, they may also be evidence of a transference resistance in play.

THAT'S NOT FAIR!

One common attitude, a customary manner of emotional response to situations that displease, is the readiness to protest, "It's not fair!" There is an implied accusation as well: "You're not fair!" An individual who is always comparing himself to others in terms of what he has, what he achieves, or the weight of his responsibilities will invariably find someone or something to generate his or her petulant complaints. These complaints often have morally justified overtones.

A parent reported the following scene that took place with his sons. He had told James and Tim that they were to rake up the yard before they could play. James was to clean up one side of the walk and Tim the other. James protested, "My side is bigger than his. It's not fair!"

Tim went on raking while James went on protesting. Tim finished his assignment and went into the house to play Nintendo. James was still stomping around the yard, protesting the unfairness of the situation. Because it was getting dark, he couldn't see what he was doing and stepped into a hole, twisting his ankle. His anger at his father escalated. James blamed him for the consequences of his own behavior. "See what you made me do!"

The sibling jealousy that had been evident since the younger Tim was born led to resentment to all authority figures who did not favor him over others. This readiness to be jealous of a therapist's other patients or of the imagined family of the therapist might be a difficult transference resistance later in life. Protests of unfairness in the world in general may become a generalized attitude of victimhood. Dealing with this resistance can be difficult inasmuch as a direct confrontation may evoke the negative transference and accusation that the therapist is not fair. Careful exploration of what the word "fair" means to the patient, may begin to uncover the resentments of childhood and the core relationship problem in which they are embedded. "I know what the word 'fair' means to me. Tell me what it means to you. Can you give me some examples?" Gradually, the complaints should narrow down to the family where the hurt and anger reside and where the analytic work can be done. When the patient perceives that the therapist is trying to understand him, the resistance will diminish. However, it is critical that the therapist maintain a stance of absolute neutrality, lest the patient feel either further victimized or validated.

Unfortunately, the demand that *life itself* be fair is a childish attitude that tends to spread to the rest of the world. Who is the omnipotent "other" in that person's mind? Is it God? Is it the government? Stirring up class envy has become a common political strategy. Who is the powerful entity, the one to bestow this fantasized fairness on him? Whose face is hidden in his protest? Mother's? Father's? Complaints of unfairness will always find some new circumstance to attack. Furthermore, envy will be spawned by the persisting attitude that everything should be even, everything should be fair. Such a disposition can only create frustration, feelings of deprivation, and bitterness.

BUT I'M ENTITLED!

Karen Horney (1950) describes what she calls "neurotic claims." An attitude of entitlement involves the participation of more than one individual. *For every entitlement, there is a claim being made on someone else.* Horney describes how these individuals feel entitled to special attention, consideration, and deference on the part of others. Of the claim, she adds, "Its non-fulfillment, then, is felt as an unfair frustration, as an offense about which we have a right to be indignant." The claim of this individual is broad and all-encompassing—that all his needs, fears, conflicts, and solutions should be respected and/or satisfied. Others exist to meet his requirements. One angry woman said of her husband, "I wasn't put on this earth just to make him feel good!" Finally, her own sense of self, of identity, gave her the courage to stand up against his unreasonable demands. Drawing support from childhood carryovers, unreasonable demands may be made in the name of fairness.

As psychotherapists, we are familiar with the attitude of entitlement that is part and parcel of the narcissistic personality disorder. It is also a familiar aspect of the masochistic personality who feels entitled to reward for her self-sacrifice. But not all attitudes of entitlement are indicative of a serious personality disorder. There is no doubt that entitlement, as a stance in life, has come to permeate our culture.

More and more attitudes of entitlement seem to be creeping into our way of thinking, our way of being in the world. Certain entitlements become enacted into law. The current political–philosophical debate between liberals and conservatives is about the role of the federal government and whether it is to provide a universal safety net for everyone. The question is asked from both sides: "How can the government manage this role without collapsing under the burden?" For every entitlement, there is a claim made on those who are to carry that burden. Our courts are crowded with lawsuits, many frivolous, arising out of the fury of not having one's entitlement claims gratified. A political–philosophical position of entitlement may draw support from an individual's personal, psychological attitude of entitlement. When a patient tries to convince his therapist of some entitlement or other, the therapist's own readiness to agree with the patient will reflect his countertransference resistance and his failure to explore the transference resistance. When the issue has political overtones, the therapist has to be especially careful not to let his or her own politics interfere with his or her neutrality. The therapist also has to monitor his reactions to the patient's politics, lest a negative or positive countertransference develop and create a resistance.

The claim of entitlement that arises from a core relationship problem is often full of righteous indignation, an anger felt to be justified and therefore "good." There is a difference between a sense of entitlement and an understandable wish that most of us might have. Wishes are often referred to as "needs," a concept that lends the wishes a degree of validity and reasonableness. We need food, water, air, and other basics of maintaining life.

An infant needs to be physically attended to. Problems arise when a wish is regarded as a need and then becomes a claim. Complaints of couples in marital therapy often consist of "I don't get my needs met!" What is at issue are the wishes that are presented as demands and entitlements.

Sticking to a stance of "I'm entitled" can endanger life itself. One woman's doctor recommended she have a hysterectomy because the likelihood of ovarian cancer was high. The woman's managed-care company, however, refused to approve payment for the procedure. They insisted she wait six months and undergo hormone treatment during that time, a treatment strongly advised against by her doctor. While she could have afforded to pay for the operation herself, she was adamant about getting what she felt entitled to from the insurance company. She would wait the six months and then they would have to pay. "I'll be darned if I'll pay for it. I'm entitled to insurance coverage for this!" Fortunately, she did not have cancer, but it could have gone the other way. Standing on her principle of entitlement, as justified as it may have been, she put her life at risk. A stubborn insistence on what one feels entitled to can prove fatal. Winning a lawsuit can never compensate for the loss of life.

NEED VERSUS DESIRE

Myerson (1981) made the distinction between need and desire as it applies to psychoanalytic psychotherapy. Putting these concepts into a developmental context, he asks, "When does a child's need *from* a parent become or not become a desire *for* the parent?" (614). The "from" reflects a passive attitude, whereas the "for" reflects a more active one. Needs that may be age-appropriate at one stage of development will be regressive at a later stage. Myerson notes that "the shift from *needs from* to *desire for* is indicative of biological maturation, but the quality and the character of the shift is influenced in a significant way by how the child's various needs are met by his parents" (161). He views the shift from the passive mode to the active mode as an important criterion for judging whether or not this shift has taken place as it should. Inappropriate parental response to this shift may lead to the child's continuing in a passive state of neediness rather than developing an active sense of himself as a desiring and responsibly aggressive person. The qualities of intrinsic power are necessary for the shift to be made—the "I am, I can, and I will." A core relationship problem arising at this place on the developmental continuum can lead to the failure to make the shift. Rather than the stance of entitlement reflecting a personality disorder, it reflects a somewhat more evolved personality, with derailment occurring in early childhood rather than babyhood or toddlerhood. Resistances in therapy will be more likely to be transference resistances rather than character resistances. In Stierlin's terms (1974), such a child may be both "id bound" and "ego bound."

Myerson stresses the importance of the therapist's responses to the passivity of the patient with respect to wishes. Will his responses to the patient's passively felt need enhance a fragile ego, or will they infantilize by reinforcing passivity and by giving credence to unrealistic wishes and fantasies? If we respond to desire, we gratify inappropriately. But if we do not respond to need, we traumatize the ego. Do we collude with the transference resistance on one hand, or do we abandon the patient at a time of fragility and vulnerability? Quite clearly, the therapist must have a clear understanding of what point on the developmental continuum the person was derailed and what are his strengths and vulnerabilities in terms of the ego functions.

A patient who has an unresolved pre-Oedipal conflict vis-à-vis the mother and who turned to the father as a substitute may sound quite Oedipal as she speaks of her wish to be wanted by her father. She plays out this wish as an adult with other men, and it is brought into the relationship with her male therapist, which creates a transference resistance. In treatment, as her work progressed, the dependent yearnings for her mother that had to be renounced emerged. A premature pseudo independence took its place alongside the grief and despair of the true little-girl self. After a disturbing message was left on the therapist's voice mail, he wondered if he should call her. On the one hand, if he did, would he be gratifying her wish to be special, as if to her father, to have him show her how much he wants her? On the other hand, if he did not call, would he be abandoning the despairing child who could not reach her mother? Would she give up, believing, once again, that it was her unreasonable neediness that drove her mother away?

In a situation like this, where the therapist is truly unsure and has to risk making an error either way, it is best to choose the response that is the least damaging and best amenable to remedying through later work. He would risk gratifying her wish in preference to abandoning her in her need and precipitating a traumatic state.

RATIONALIZATION AS A RESISTANCE

Rationalization is one of the higher-level—i.e., more mature—mechanisms of defense. It may be used to cover up or justify an act or an idea that is unreasonable or illogical. Rationalization is sometimes used more widely as a way to avoid taking responsibility for one's way of being in the world. At this point, it becomes a resistance. Behind its use is an attitude of "Don't blame me. That's just the way I am." It denies that one has dynamics and motivations that cause problems in life. "You'll have to accept me for who I am" is the usual retort when the individual is criticized, perhaps for being "lazy" and for the problems he is causing himself and his wife by his failure to get his income tax filed, for instance. He speaks of his "laziness" as though it were a trait derived from his DNA. Another example of labeling and rationalizing problem-making behavior is the response that "I'm just a procrastinator."

While these social labels are used to ward off criticism, they also cover over the conflicted motives that are active beneath them. The underlying hostility and aggression is hidden even from oneself. He feels no guilt. There may even be a certain amount of pleasure, of hidden gratification at getting away with being bad. It is easier to wallow in excuses than tackle the difficult psychological work of confronting the hidden motives. There doesn't seem to be anything to gain. The here-and-now relationship in which the story is being played out is obviously unpleasant much of the time, yet he is not moved to wonder what his part in the bickering might be. His aggression is acted out in passive-aggressive and devious ways that allow for denial and rationalization. The overt "I'm just lazy" excuse may be concealing the covert "I refuse to do what you want." The refusal itself may be a way to hold on to power and control in the relationship. The partner may be labeled unreasonable should she complain—which she does a lot. Her complaining simply leads to her being called a "nag."

In therapy, his rationalization blocks any attempt to understand the "laziness" as a behavior that follows its own scenario, one that involves another person either in the present or from the past. It is motivated behavior. It doesn't happen all by itself. His very use of the term is a way to control the therapy and the therapist. At this point, rationalization becomes a transference resistance. Behind it is the angry and oppositional "no" of the newly individuating child. The power struggle that may be set up with the parent at this point may feel too dangerous to play out openly. Either he will be punished, perhaps with the loss of his mother's love, or his refusal to give in to her will harm her in some way. The potential destructiveness of his angry aggression sends it underground. He may devise a strategy of overt compliance with covert defiance—a pattern often seen in passive-aggressive behaviors. The core relationship problem emerges as he is derailed from the developmental continuum and blocked from healthy, normal individuation. The compliance–defiance pattern will be enacted with the therapist, perhaps when it comes time to pay the bill. "Gee, I"m sorry, I keep forgetting your check. I've always had such a bad memory." The therapist may react consciously or unconsciously to the power issue, feeling under the passive control of the patient. This countertransference reaction must be attended to privately, lest the therapist act out his anger against the patient. The oppositional two-year-old and the angry mother will, in effect, be in the room. Because there is a cohesive self, exploration, uncovering, and interpretation can be undertaken with this individual. Its enactment with the therapist must be confronted.

The use of rationalization as a resistance can also be a defense against the felt danger of making a mistake. He may ruefully tell the therapist, "I'm just a procrastinator," but deep down he may believe, "If I don't act, I can't do anything wrong." There is anxiety behind this defensive excuse. On the face of it, this is ridiculous because he will get in trouble for the avoidance itself. The harsh critical voice of his mother finds its way into every situation, and fear of her caustic, wounding words may lead to the individual's fear of taking action. Attributing the same hurtful potential to the therapist, the rationalized refusal to act, perhaps to speak his own mind, is his way of making sure he is safe in the relationship. It is a transference resistance.

The fear of doing something wrong is a close relative of the belief in the mythical, nonexistent "it." If he had done it right, whatever "it" was, surely his mother would have always been warm and supportive. Perhaps he can't let himself see her as she really was and still is: a bitter, angry woman who took all her unhappiness out on him. The complexities of his fears and defenses may, at first, only be manifest in his use of rationalization for passive inaction. He tells his therapist, "I can't help it. I'm just lazy."

Other such labeling rationalizations are encountered with patients. "I'm a control freak" both acknowledges the wish to control but, at the same time, denies responsibility for it. There is a "take it or leave it" quality to the assertion. "I just have high standards" may be a justification for a controlling perfectionism that ruins all relationships. Beneath this may be her mythical "it." Being perfect is her "it." It is also one she demands of others—they must do it right or she will turn against them, as her mother turned against her. If she brings this into the therapy as a transference resistance, failure to bring it into the light of examination may well lead to an abrupt ending to the treatment when she feels the therapist has been less than perfect. This particular dynamic is consistent with the reaction of the narcissistic personality disorder when the idealizing transference is broken because of a failure of empathy on the part of the therapist. Once again, it is important to be clear whether the resistance comes out of a character disorder or whether it arises from a later place on the developmental continuum, such as the process of individuation.

Another rationalizing label is that of "workaholic." Does the person use work to avoid intimacy? Work can fill up the void of aloneness. The excitement of work can even act as a temporary antidepressant. Thus, it has a manic quality to it. Discomfort and anxiety are likely to be stirred up by examining his behavior too closely, so it will be easier to cling to the rationalization for his being alone. In this case, the danger behind the resistance is inherent in the relationship. What is he attributing to the therapist that necessitates a detachment in order to be safe? Exploring that detachment can uncover the dangers that originally led to schizoid or schizoid-like defenses that now hide behind the label "workaholic."

Sometimes a person who is hostile and hurtful to the other will seem to be upset at the other's negative reaction. "I was only kidding," he insists. "I thought you could take a joke." Not only does he deny his dark side, he accuses the other of being stupid or crazy for accurately perceiving and reacting to his hostility. He tells others, "I'm just a kidder." He enjoys hiding behind the comic mask. At one level, he denies to himself that he is really petty and mean. At an unconscious level, he is still getting even for all the times his father ridiculed him. But his anger is misdirected and he is taking his hurt out on the rest of the world—probably including his therapist. Direct confrontation will activate his belittling of the therapist, but the rationalization must be confronted and be related directly to what he is doing in the therapeutic relationship. Confrontation entails more than a simplistic pointing of the finger and accusing the individual of rationalizing what he doesn't want to admit.

Confrontation of the Rationalization by Aggressive Inquiry

What makes these rationalizations a resistance is that they are ego-syntonic—no more than quaint foibles that should just be accepted by others. After all, no one is perfect. A useful approach to working with them is to insist on their exploration as soon as they appear. It is important not to let these usually flip remarks go by without inquiry. They are clues to what lies beneath them. To "I'm a control freak," one can move right into asking for the details. "What is it that you want to control?" "What might happen if you were not able to control that?" An unrelenting pursuit of what lies behind the defensive need to control should point the way to the core relationship problem, and to where the individual was derailed from the developmental continuum. Perhaps what will be uncovered is an insecure attachment and the felt need to control the object so as not to be abandoned. The therapist can never jump to conclusions.

The same approach is applicable to any of these postures described by the patient who is unwittingly revealing more about himself than he realizes. It is up to the therapist to cut through the resistance—the denial of significance of what the individual has just said about himself. This relentless pursuit of the hidden dynamic is likely to evoke anxiety in the patient. How he reacts to the anxiety will give more information with which the therapist can work. As the rationalization becomes less ego-syntonic, the observing ego may kick into action. This style of aggressive inquiry is exemplified by the verbatim case study in chapter 13.

Of course, the usual caveat applies here as well. If at any time it is obvious that this aggressive line of inquiry is a threat to a fragile underlying character structure, the therapist will reassess the rationalization. Perhaps it is a character resistance protesting the cohesion of the self. As with all patients, the therapist must always be ready to assess where the patient is on the *empathy–anxiety* gradient at any moment and be prepared to shift approach if necessary.

The conversion of the resistance from ego-syntonic to ego-dystonic and the mobilization of the observing ego will dissolve the resistance so that the work can progress. C. S. Lewis apparently understands this premise. In Lewis's (2001) *The Screwtape Letters,* Screwtape writes to his nephew Wormwood of a potential denizen of Hell: "You must bring him to a condition in which he can practice self-examination for an hour without discovering any of those facts about himself, which are perfectly clear to anyone who has ever lived in the same house with him or worked in the same office." We might add, or whoever has been his psychotherapist.

Some destructive motives are so all-consuming that they become resistances in and of themselves. We can predict that the relevant core-relationship problem and its manifestations in the transference are likely to be difficult.

11

Motives as Resistance

VENGEANCE

Sometimes an individual's dominant motive can become his life motif, the central theme of what moves him. It even comes to describe him. He is a vengeful man. The wish for revenge locks a person into the past, holding him hostage to a relationship that was hurtful and humiliating. It is a deadly dynamic that leads to endless wars and persecutions, to family feuds and gang murders.

Issues of war and peace are often mentioned in terms more appropriate to the adolescent game of "chicken." Asked about an exchange between the president of the United States and the secretary general of the USSR, a reporter inquired, "Who blinked first?" Being "dissed"—shown disrespect—requires retaliation. Warring gangs in the inner cities of America accept this as one of their basic principles. The dread of "losing face" is not a concern of Oriental nations alone. When a person or a group feels offended and humiliated, injured or insulted, there is a wish to punish the offender. There seems to be a belief that by turning the tables, the humiliation can be erased.

While *undoing* is a defense mechanism that eliminates feelings of conscious or unconscious remorse by the use of a magical gesture that annuls the forbidden act, it can also be used to defend against the intolerable feelings evoked by the act of someone else on the self. It involves the magical assumption that the original event and its consequences can be undone. Sometimes vengeance is seen as the only way to eradicate the rage and unbearable frustration of helplessness. Unfortunately, living with these toxic emotions day after day, or year after year, leaves little room for anything positive. Nothing else seems significant. On the news, we hear about a family whose life for the past eleven years has been organized around their determination to see that the man who murdered their son is executed. The mother believes that when this finally happens, she will be able to get on with her life. She has been in limbo all that time, neither living nor dead. The murdered man's newborn son spent the first and most formative years of his life with this retaliation serving as the family's top priority, a priority that tended to push out all lesser ones. Who will he become as a consequence of this warping of the fabric of his family? Who might he have become with other values taking precedence? One may agree that capital punishment is appropriate for this kind of murder, but the obsessive need for revenge has another dynamic—it becomes what life itself is all about.

In Alan Dershowitz's novel *Just Revenge* (1999), he looks into the heart of a Holocaust survivor for whom there can be no rest until he has taken revenge against the man responsible for the deaths of his family in the concentration camp. There is no rest, no making a new life. The seeker of revenge is held hostage to his own painful drama.

A vivid example of the destructiveness of untamed vengeance can be found in Greek mythology. Medea was a princess and sorceress who helped Jason and his Argonauts obtain the magical Golden Fleece. But when Medea is publicly humiliated by the unfaithfulness of her husband, Jason, her murderous fury dooms their sons, who become instruments with which to punish their father. We read regularly in our newspapers of present-day Medeas or their male counterparts. They are the rejected and abandoned wives or husbands who take revenge against their mate by murdering their children. This terrible failure of what is the ideal of maternal instinct may be difficult for some to comprehend. On the other hand, vengeance may be sought on behalf of a child, such as the case of the woman who was sentenced to prison for killing the man who had molested her son. When the drive for revenge is acted out, judgment with respect to consequences is irrelevant at that moment.

In a somewhat lighter vein, we hear one character in the movie *The First Wives Club* say to the group, all of whom have been left by their husbands for other women, "Don't get even! Get everything!" Not only did these women want to punish the men, they also wanted to undo the humiliation of being cast away. More than three hundred years ago, English author William Cosgrove wrote: "Heaven has no rage like love to hatred turned,/Nor hell a fury like a woman scorned."

These "first wives" were consumed with a wish for vengeance. Regardless of how sympathetic their position might be, they were hostage to the wish. They would not be free to make a new, satisfying relationship. They fed one another's sense of a guilt-free moral righteousness.

VINDICTIVE TRIUMPH

How many men and women who were unpopular nerds in high school go to their twentieth reunion for the express purpose of parading their success, to rub it in the faces of the jocks and beauty queens who rejected them back then? Would that they all could declare the ultimate triumph of ex-nerd Bill Gates. Karen Horney (1950) describes the drive toward *vindictive triumph* as the most destructive of the paths to the search for glory. She says that it may be closely linked with the drive for actual achievement and success, but

> if so, its chief aim is to put others to shame, or defeat them through one's very success; or to attain power, by rising to prominence, to inflict suffering upon them—mostly of a humiliating kind. On the other hand, the drive for excelling may be relegated to fantasy, and the need for a vindictive triumph then manifests itself mainly in often irresistible, mostly unconscious impulses to frustrate, outwit, or defeat others in personal relations. I call this drive "vindictive triumph" because the motivating force stems from impulses to take revenge for humiliations suffered in childhood—impulses which are reinforced during later neurotic development. (27)

Horney notes that most people are unaware of this motive or of its strength. However, for others, it is out in the open and "then it becomes the barely disguised mainspring of life."

When the chief aim of success is to put others to shame, there can be little satisfaction in one's work when this raging energy is what drives an individual. While this form of vengeance may not seem destructive on the face of it, with the underlying motive to destroy, to hurt, or to humiliate, healthy motives based on love, creative interests, or a wish to make a productive contribution to the world cannot exist. Perhaps they never even developed. Not only are individual lives compromised by vengeful preoccupation. The larger world is also worse off.

Developmental Derailment and Resistance

The drive for vengeance, the wish to take revenge, can erupt all along the developmental continuum when frustration and humiliation are so intense as to override any preexisting positive attitude toward the offending individual. Indeed, when the hurt is experienced as betrayal, there is a mental destruction of the offender's goodness. Where there has been a more primitive good–bad split in the image of the object, the interpersonal dynamic described by Kohut (1971)—when there is a failure of the idealizing transference and a turning back to the grandiose self—takes place in the relationship in question. The narcissistic rage annihilates the good object.

On the other hand, the child may have achieved the capacity for ambivalence, the coexistence of positive and negative feelings toward the object. If the betrayal is experienced as egregious enough, the positive side of the ambivalence is repressed and only the negative remains to fuel the drive for vengeance. At some point toward the end of successful therapy, he or she should be able to retrieve the positive feelings toward the hurtful other of childhood.

An example of such a perceived betrayal is that of the little girl whose special relationship with her adoring father led her to believe that she had triumphed over her mother in the triangle. This is often the fantasy of the girl's "Oedipal triumph." In this case, the father left the mother for another woman and left his daughter behind when he went to live with the woman. The depths of the felt betrayal of the promise and expectation of that specialness led to a rage that the little girl carried into her adult life. While she could not act out her revenge on her father directly, she did with other men. Once she had made herself important to them emotionally, she would drop them without explanation, leaving them as mystified and hurt as she was when her father left. This is an example of how the motive for revenge can arise after separation and individuation, at the time of the emergence of the Oedipal triangle in the child's development. If she goes to a male therapist, the likelihood of her playing this out with him is great. The transference resistance will be manifest in her attempts to make herself special to him, perhaps through seductiveness. If she believes she has succeeded in doing so, she may end her therapy abruptly, taking her therapist by surprise. He may have misinterpreted her apparently positive attitude toward him as a manifestation of a good therapeutic alliance. If she is attractive, his countertransference resistance might be manifest in his narcissistic gratification in believing himself to be so special to her. Treatment with a woman therapist would reveal the other side of the Oedipal dynamics (see Table 11.1, from Horner 1994) and would preclude the acting-out resistance she would play with any male therapist.

Determination of the core relationship problem as it relates to the time of developmental derailment will be important in the therapy. Will the patient be able to maintain a therapeutic alliance in the face of disappointment with the therapist or not? The more primitive patient will not. With the more evolved individual, despite transference attributions, he or she is likely to be able to manage disappointment and work with interpretation. With the more primitive patient, the rage toward the offending other

Table 11.1 Steps Necessary to Resolve the Oedipus Complex

Steps	Opposite-Sex Parent	Same-Sex Parent
1. Uncovering		
acknowledge wish, fantasy, or desire	to have sexually and/or be the preferred object	to defeat in competition and to displace; to murder
understand fear associated with the wish	loss of control	punishment (e.g., castration or withdrawal of love); guilt
understand negative affect associated with frustration	anger; feelings of betrayal; sense of failure or inadequacy; sadness, yearning	humiliation; envy
2. Working Through		
insight into how conflicts are played out a) in present-day life b) in the transference	interference with heterosexual relationships	interference with achievement of goals and ambitions
3. Resolution		
renunciation of the wish	to have sexually and/or be the preferred object	to defeat in competition and to displace
acceptance of parents as real people	without the need to idealize or disparage	without the need to idealize or disparage
acknowledgment of identifications	with opposite-sex parent without endangerment of gender identity and/ or the ego-ideal	with same-sex parent without endangerment of the ego-ideal
neutralization of drive	desexualization of affection toward parent of opposite sex	de-aggressivization of strivings for success and achievement
redirection of strivings	to new love object reunion of sex and affection without guilt or anxiety	toward ambitions strivings for success and achievement without guilt or anxiety
4. Termination		
therapist is perceived in realistic terms as adult equal	patient withdraws emotional investment in treatment and redirects it toward his/ her real life	patient actively takes full responsibility for own life

will be generic. With the more evolved patient, the rage and wish for vengeance remain specific to the individual or individuals who committed the original affront or their direct derivatives, such as in the example of the young girl above.

With the more primitive patient, resistance will be in the order of character resistances that defend against the failure of primitive defenses and loss of self-cohesion or emergence of an anaclitic depression. With the more evolved individual, transference resistances will dominate and will have to be perceived and worked with by the therapist. One of the most difficult resistances will be the patient's insistence on the righteousness of his vengeful wishes and attempts to convince the therapist of this righteousness and of his goodness. In this respect, he is like the "good boy." The dark side is split off and repressed. The intransigence of the motive may frustrate the therapist. His or her reactions to that frustration require personal attention, lest they be acted out, reenacting the early betrayal of trust.

Horney reflects on the feelings of being abused and thus entitled to having others make up for the injuries perpetrated on him. In dreams, he may present himself as being ruined beyond repair and hence entitled to having all his wishes fulfilled. She notes that in order to understand these vindictive elements, the therapist must explore the factor of the patient's feelings of having been abused. Whether or not this posture is a manifestation of the narcissistic entitlement of the narcissistic or masochistic personality disorders will have different implications for the treatment process than if they are specific to the "crime" in question. The fantasized repair of the damage to himself that would be achieved through revenge contributes to the felt need for revenge. Exploring what he feels or believes to have been damaged in him becomes a significant aspect of the work. The potential for shame will contribute to the resistance to the work and to the therapist as an agent of the work.

SPITE

A child's self-image, the beliefs she has about herself, in large part come from the picture of herself as she believes her mother or father saw her. In other words, the child is *defined by the other.* The child who grows up feeling devalued and humiliated by parents builds up enormous anger in reaction to their negativity. But she also believes that their judgment is correct because they are viewed as all-knowing and all-powerful. The child who is told, "You ruined my life by being born," goes through life with a firm belief that she has no right to exist. And she will behave accordingly, submerging herself in all relationships, including that with her therapist. At the same time—feeling devalued and humiliated—these feelings may build up over the early years to lead to a wish to get even by hurting the parents' images of themselves. She may make herself a weapon and do things publicly that will embarrass them. This is the essence of spite. Spite is a particular form of vengeance. It has no purpose other than to thwart the other person or harm him in some way. The phrase, "Don't bite off your nose to spite your face" sums it up. When he was angry at his mother, one little boy would go to his room and smash his toys. Spite, as a self-destructive form of aggression against another, must be named for what it is in the treatment. A transference resistance may be acted out against the therapist in the same spiteful manner as with parents. Sometimes suicide may be the ultimate act of spite, which announces the failure of her parents as parents to the world at large. She "blows the cover" of their public goodness. She shames them as they once shamed her.

"SAY YOU'RE SORRY"

Another dynamic that comes from a posture of being damaged in some way is the insistence on an apology from parents for real or imagined hurts of childhood. Sometimes with the encouragement of a well-meaning friend or of a misguided therapist, an individual may decide to "confront" the parents with their failures or wrongdoings as parents. From a therapy standpoint, it is important that the person look behind the impulse or intention to do so, to ask about the wish he or she would carry into the confrontation. The wish may be fully conscious or not. Sometimes, he or she will say of the mother, "I just want her to say she's sorry," to apologize for whatever the festering wound may be. For the wish to succeed, the patient must show how hurt, wounded, or damaged she is. Otherwise, there would be no justification for the confrontation. Whether subtle or more obvious, the message is "see what you did to me."

As in the case of a drive for revenge or of spiteful behavior, the individual makes of herself or himself a walking reproach, a constant reminder that the parent has failed. These are powerful motives for one to remain in a state of misery and failure. In psychotherapy, this person will unconsciously sabotage productive change. No amount of therapy will bring real progress as long as the desire to remain the same dominates one's approach to life and relationships. Vengefulness, spitefulness, and blaming others as motives or as life motifs become major resistances to the work of treatment and to the therapist, whose goal is seen as bringing about positive change and progress. This perceived demand by the therapist (Friedman 1997) will have to be frustrated, just as the individual's needs and wishes were frustrated in childhood. The therapist's ability to see and understand the patient's acting out in the transference should prevent a countertransference acting-out, colluding with the patient's reenactment of the childhood dynamic vis-à-vis the parent.

Part of the "Say you're sorry" scenario is the wish to make the parents feel guilty, to damage their view of themselves as parents and as people— in short, to make them suffer. Although the individual would loudly deny his wish to hurt his parents, the wish to make the other feel guilty is a covert form of aggression. It is intended to produce pain. It is the hidden "dark side" of the patient's morally superior victim-self.

Tony's suicide fantasy fits into this category. He reveled in the image of killing himself at his parents' front door, imagining their shock and horror at discovering his bloody body. As a member of a therapy group, it was clear that he was continually competing with the others for the position of most-aggrieved victim. Yet, because he was passive and wore his suffering on his sleeve, his therapist made the mistake of taking an empathic and supporting approach instead of confronting him about his behavior—a behavior that was hardly passive but was undoubtedly the covert and perverse expression of hateful aggression.

When a confrontation of the parents evokes their apologies for all the ways in which they failed the individual as a child, the accuser's sense of his own goodness as innocent victim seems affirmed in righteous anger. Finally he has been vindicated. He no longer has to feel guilty about his wish to strike out and hurt his parent or parents. At the same time, he can maintain an arrogant belief in his own moral superiority.

More rarely, the anger that has simmered and eaten away at the son or daughter for most of their lives may be quieted once the parent admits his or her failure and asks for forgiveness. In a more evolved individual who has achieved the developmental task of the capacity for ambivalence, the soothing away of the anger allows buried feelings of love to emerge once more. The apology repairs the felt breech between child and parent, dissipating, at least temporarily, the chronic depression that resulted from the loss of loving connection. Even with this ideal outcome of the confrontation, the person must then take responsibility for real change and must face the reality about the part that he, himself, has played in his own misery.

Unfortunately, the ideal wished-for outcome of confronting the parents who failed to live up to what the child wished for rarely comes about. Most likely, the parents' own version of their reality will not allow for any change in their view of themselves or their behavior. More likely, they will feel unjustly accused, and the son or daughter will only feel guilt and a sense of badness, a feeling about the self that is likely to intensify with the frustration and rage brought on from the confrontation gone wrong.

The therapist who recommends that the patient confront the parent or parents is acting out a countertransference resistance and is colluding with the patient's resistances to self-discovery. Perhaps she identifies with the wounded child of the patient and acts out her own parent dynamics through him. He serves as a proxy for her disowned hostility toward her parent or parents. This is not empathy. With empathy, the boundary between self and other is maintained. In this kind of identification, the boundary is lost. Perhaps the therapist is frustrated at the tenacity with which the patient clings to the victim posture. Sending him to his parents may be acting out an unconscious wish to get rid of him and, thus, to get rid of the feelings of powerlessness.

An ongoing self-analysis and containment of the negative feelings stirred up in working with this kind of patient is essential if the therapist is to be able to do the necessary uncovering and confrontation of the patient's maladaptive life strategies. Up to the present, those strategies have been unconscious and ego-syntonic. When they have been made conscious and rendered ego-dystonic, the work can get under way. Analysis of the transference resistance will be an essential ingredient for this outcome.

"TEACHER'S PET" AND THE NEED TO BE SPECIAL

One of the most persistent motives that will block progress in psychotherapy is that of the wish to be special to the idealized authority figure. The gratification of achieving the wish counteracts the problems it may cause. The path from being mother's favorite child, to daddy's golden girl, to third-grade teacher's pet, to special assistant (and confidante) to one's thesis advisor, to being the special employee in the eyes of one's supervisor, to being protégé of one's mentor is an unbroken path of sought-after and successfully achieved specialness.

One of the costs of becoming the successful "teacher's pet" in the world at large is that the person has to remain a child in those relationships—an adorable child, a clever child, but a child nevertheless. She may have a troublesome feeling of resentment at the power the other has, even though it may be used for her benefit. The discomfort evoked by the conflict may motivate her to consult a psychotherapist.

There are prominent movie and television stars whose cultivated charm rests on their being cute and adorable. One wonders what they will be like in middle age and beyond. The image of "Baby Jane" played by Bette Davis comes to mind. While certainly not as grotesque as Baby Jane, the perennial golden girl is also stunted in her development until and unless she is able to relinquish the rewards that come by virtue of being an adorable child in exchange for being an adult in the world of adults. Otherwise she does not age well. Should such an individual consult a psychotherapist, this posture will have to be treated as a major transference resistance.

Another cost is that of true friendship. Friendship is a relationship of peers, of equals. In the peer group, the child has to give up the aura of specialness and its rewards. Little children on the playground are amazingly perceptive. They quickly sense the attitude of the child who has to be special and reject him or her.

As a child, this individual may have managed to preserve her sense of specialness in another way, such as becoming the mascot of a team (but not a player), or even acting as a leader through some special talent that sets her apart. But in a world of peers, competitiveness will usually arise in some fashion. The individual who cannot tolerate losing the position of specialness as a result of a competitive loss will probably stick to the game where she is a tried-and-true winner. As an adult, she may feel frustrated by her inability to pursue her healthier goals. Best daughter. Best student. Best employee. And, of course, best therapy patient. Although she carries herself above the group, she may yearn for the rewards of true friendship. She may be motivated to consult a therapist with the presenting complaint, "I don't know why I don't have any friends."

Questions about a new patient's history of friendships will elicit information about her ability or inability to maintain a truly peer relationship. Indications of pathological narcissism, of insecure attachment, of Oedipal defeat, or of Oedipal triumph may become evident from such a line of exploration. The drive to be special may emerge at any one of these places on the developmental continuum, and it will be embedded in the core relationship problem.

Grandiose Self

If a grandiose self defensive structure is manifest in the posture of specialness, character resistances that protect the cohesion of the self will be evident in treatment and will have to managed in such a way as not to traumatize the patient.

False Self

Insecurity of early attachment may lead to the construction of a false self whose aim is to maintain the connection with the object through some strategy ensuring specialness. If she is special, she will not be abandoned, possibly to experience object loss and emergence of an anaclitic depression. A transference resistance that strives to re-create the false self connection by means of finding a way to be special to the therapist will create an impasse in treatment. Strengths and vulnerabilities of the patient will inform the therapist as where he can interpret the transference resistance or where he must provide a place of safety for the true self to emerge.

Conflicted Drive Toward Individuation

The drive toward individuation and the fear of object loss or loss of the object's love may pinpoint the rapprochement crisis as the point of derailment as well as the core relationship problem. Strategies to ensure specialness are created in order to prevent the disruption of the positive connection to the mother. These strategies will be played out and stand as a transference resistance in psychotherapy.

Oedipal Conflict

The striving toward specialness may also come out of the attempt to make up for the humiliation of an Oedipal defeat or out of an unwillingness to give up the gratification of an Oedipal victory. At this point on the developmental continuum, although there may be residual rapprochement issues that will emerge in treatment, they will be intricately woven into the Oedipal issues. The transference resistance, as it may appear in attempts to win the therapist's special affection, can be safely interpreted. The verbatim case presentation in chapter 13 dramatically illuminates this situation.

While the "presenting problem" may be in terms of a troublesome symptom, the therapist may soon discover that the symptom is also a resistance. Deciphering the core relationship problem in which the symptom is embedded will be crucial, lest the therapist become embroiled in a transference–countertransference impasse.

12

Symptoms as Resistance

THE EATING "DISORDERS"

Just as motivation, an intrinsic aspect of an individual's psychology, can become a resistance, so may a symptom that is the result of conflicts about interpersonal relationships. A fever may be a symptom of a wide variety of physical illnesses, all the way from a sore throat or the flu to appendicitis, tuberculosis, lupus, ulcerative colitis, Hodgkin's disease, and many more. The elevated body temperature is not the illness. It is a sign that illness exists. From the perspective of a medical model, psychological symptoms are viewed as the illness rather than as a sign that psychological illness exists. A psychology of the mind will seek to find the underlying causes of the psychological symptom. This applies, in particular, to the so-called eating disorders.

Once the symptom has become an obsession, which is not an illness but a defense mechanism, its potential to be a resistance in psychotherapy is magnified. The obsession has been described earlier in this book as a kind of mental magnet that draws all thought, feeling, and attention away from where the conflict really lies—most often embedded in the core relationship problem. The obsession is a diversionary tactic. It focuses the attention somewhere else—on food, for example—providing a magical solution to the relationship conflict. Of course, it does not fix the problem because the temporary success of the magical solution is an illusion—and in some more serious cases, a delusion. It shifts the locus of the anxiety away from the internal conflicts that are so troubling and seemingly unresolvable to the solution the individual's creative mind has designed. The illusion, the defense mechanism, becomes an obsession. The obsession may be about eating and weight. The underlying source of the symptom is the disturbed pattern of interpersonal relationships. This pattern can sometimes be characterized as a *need–fear dilemma*. As one can imagine, if a very small child is caught between his age-appropriate need for his mother and a fear of her, he is faced with an unsolvable dilemma.

THE APPROACH–AVOIDANCE CONFLICT

An *approach–avoidance conflict* exists when a person is simultaneously attracted to and repelled by a single goal object (Munn et al. 1972). As the person moves closer to the goal on the basis of the attraction or desirability of the object, the strength of the repelling force grows, reaching a point at which an avoidant turning away from the goal or object is mobilized. Then, as the individual gets farther and farther from what is desired, anxiety is reduced and attraction, wish, or desire asserts itself once again. Again, the direction of movement is reversed. Obviously, this situation may pertain to a relationship conflict, manifested by both a wish for and a fear of the object or of the relationship set up as it has been historically established.

Even more troublesome is the existence of a *double approach–avoidance conflict* that exists when the individual has both positive and negative attitudes toward *two* goals that have come to be experienced or perceived as mutually exclusive, with the same opposing forces operating in relation to both goals or both objects. This relational dilemma may come into being at various levels of psychological development.

Stage of Differentiation

During the earliest stage of differentiation, inherent strivings of the self may be accompanied by the threat of object-loss and a consequent loss of cohesion of the self or a further falling back to an anaclitic depression. Movement back toward the object may restore the sense of cohesion and connection at the cost of the loss of the emerging identity as a separate self. This would constitute an early derailment from the developmental continuum and the consolidation of a core relationship problem characterized by the failure of the mother to provide the holding environment described by Winnicott with disruption of the child's sense of going-on-being. The core relationship problem would entail a lack of basic trust and defenses that would protect the child from the effects of the vagaries of maternal care. Schizoid defenses and a good innate intelligence may permit the development of the autonomous ego functions that would enable him to be in the world. If the therapist were to create an atmosphere of trust, the individual might move toward him or her, but wariness at his perceived failures would reactivate the schizoid flight from the connection. Character resistances would protect the cohesion of the self.

In the case of the most severe disruptions at this stage of development, language may not yet have developed to the point where the child's inner experience can be organized symbolically. Instead, there may be wide fluctuations of affect and disruption of smooth bodily functions such as might affect the gastrointestinal symptom. With no words to connect the bodily experiences with a specific affect, such as fear or depression, the child may later be viewed as alexithymic.

Rickles (1986) describes the propensity of these people to fall ill medically when subjected to environmental stress, disappointment, object loss, or humiliations. He views alexithymia as a "subcategory of self disorders." He reports how psychosomatic problems often take the form of a paucity of affective description and intrapsychic awareness. The word "alexithymic" means "without words for feelings." They have a tendency to think in operational, descriptive, or task-oriented terms without reference to feelings or interpersonal meanings. Their object relations are described as rigidly conventional and seem to be based on seeing others as stereotypes and "reduplications" of themselves. Capacity for the empathic experiencing of objects as individuals is almost totally missing. Rickles notes that because of a split and subsequent defect in self-experience as agent and self as observer, the individual cannot see this connection and cannot use defense/resistance oriented psychoanalysis in a constructive way.

Rapprochement

An unsuccessful resolution of the rapprochement phase of the separation–individuation process leaves the person both drawn to and repelled by movement closer to and away from the mother. The dependent wish is countered by a fear of engulfment or a loss of autonomy. It may also be countered by negative, hurtful memories of being close to an ambivalent mother who was also loving and caring. A need–fear dilemma is created by this situation.

The wish for autonomy is countered by fear of loss of the object or the object's love, which engenders intense separation anxiety or depression. The less than good-enough mothering earlier on left an insecurity about taking the next step forward. If the child moves back for refueling, which mother will be there to greet her—the loving, caring one, or the sometimes hurtful one? This is an example of how problems at one stage of development lead to a compromised ability to negotiate the next stage.

In therapy, the need–fear dilemma will be brought to the treatment relationship. There may be a resistance to a dependent relationship—a form of transference resistance. One can most often assume that the attachment process and organization of a cohesive self went well enough that there is less likelihood of a character resistance, although the therapist always has to be aware that, under a situation of regression, manifestations of an insecure attachment may surface.

Oedipal Stage

The Oedipal stage of development shows the child moving out of a dyadic relationship structure to a triangular one. The child may experience herself in a lose-lose situation: if she chooses mother, she loses father, losing his love and developmental support, or fearing his anger and punishment. If, on the other hand, she chooses father, she fears the loss of mother's love. In addition, sexual anxieties associated to closeness with him add to the need–fear dilemma. *A heightened ambivalence toward both mother and father is a major contributing factor in the situation of a double approach–avoidance situation.* The wish for mother may be countered by its regressive implications in addition to anxieties associated with being close to her. The wish for father may also be countered by a fear of his closeness in situations where he sexualizes the relationship with excessive attention to how she looks.

The confluence of the pre-Oedipal and Oedipal levels intensifies the double approach–avoidance situation. There is an overlap with the later rapprochement period and the Oedipal stage. Oedipal anxieties aggravate rapprochement anxieties, and vice versa.

COMPROMISE FORMATION

The seriously troubled relationships with parents in early childhood create huge anxieties over feelings and impulses, needs and desires. A variety of defenses are erected to contend with fears and anxiety. A complex compromise formation brings all of these together into a single symptom.

For hundreds of years, the language of ancient Egypt had been a riddle to scholars. Then, in 1799, an officer of Napoleon's engineering corps unearthed what has come to be known as the Rosetta stone near the mouth of the Nile River. On it was a decree by Ptolemy V, carved around 196 B.C. The inscription appeared in three languages; one was the then-mysterious hieroglyphics of the ancient Egyptians, but one of the remaining two was ancient Greek. By translating the Greek and using it as a guide, scholars were able to begin deciphering these ancient hieroglyphics.

Today, the term "Rosetta stone" denotes that which holds the key to understanding puzzling situations. By approaching the symptom—the compromise formation—as the Rosetta stone, the key to understanding the patient, we are able to discover the nature of the underlying complex core relationship problem. If we understand bulimia as a complex compromise formation, we will not be caught up in the obsession along with the patient. Her problem is not about food or about weight. It is about the unresolved double approach–avoidance conflicts with respect to her relationships with both father and mother. The symptom is, in essence, a metaphor for the highly conflicted interpersonal situation. It is for this reason that dealing with the transference and its resistances is central to the treatment of bulimia, inasmuch as the intrapsychic conflicts and the defenses against their distress will be manifest in the treatment relationship. Bulimia is, first and foremost, a disorder of *human relationship.*

BULIMIA AND TRANSFERENCE RESISTANCE

The double-approach avoidance conflict leads to an obsessive fear of making the wrong decision. The obsession may take one of a number of avenues for its expression. At this point, it becomes a *symptom.* Any decision has an inherent wrongness to it. A stage-appropriate interpretation of the underlying developmental and relationship dilemma is necessary to a resolution of the impasse and a subsiding of the obsessional symptomatology. In psychotherapy, once the emphasis is placed on the *interpersonal* nature of the core conflict in which the obsession is embedded, both patient and therapist will be freed from the helplessness and frustration of perseverating ideation and behavior, allowing the analytic work to proceed. The treatment itself will still carry all the difficulties of dealing with disturbed relationship patterns, both in terms of transference and countertransference resistances, but at least both parties will be able to feel some movement rather than the impotence of being caught in the obsession itself. The transference resistance to a commitment to therapy and the therapist will be a manifestation of the approach–avoidance pattern relating to one parent or the other. The countertransference frustration of the situation may provoke negatively charged behavior that will be a replication of the negativity of the hurtful parent.

I also see bulimia as a failed schizoid defense, a situation in which the pull of the exciting objects—the pre-Oedipal mother and the Oedipal father—was, and continues to be, too powerful to deny. As with all patients with schizoid defenses, establishing an emotional connection in the treatment is of paramount importance. From the bulimic patient's perspective, however, this is exactly what is to be avoided most. She vacillates between connection and disconnection, often confusing the therapist as to the nature of the transference of the moment. He must walk a very narrow line of neutrality. Exhibiting either positive or negative feelings toward the patient will confirm her fears that he is as dangerous as were mother or father. The countertransference reaction to the double-binding "come close, stay away" will stir up the therapist's own issues with respect to the mixed message. Dealing with these privately, the therapist stays steady and neutral. The therapist's annoyance stirs up the patient's fears of mother's unpredictable angers. The therapist's support or encouragement stirs up the patient's fears of father's seductiveness. Interpretations fail when they miss where the patient is with respect to pre-Oedipal dangers versus Oedipal dangers.

Because of the complicated transference issues and the sensitivity demanded of the therapist, it is no wonder that many prefer to work directly with the symptoms with cognitive-behavioral strategies that may provide a built-in distancing factor, protecting the therapeutic dyad from the excitement–deprivation–rage pattern characteristic of the bulimic relationship. As one such patient concluded, "isolating the self is better; the real self is too vulnerable and too scared."

THE CORE RELATIONSHIP PROBLEM
AND ANOREXIA NERVOSA

In his book *Starving to Death in a Sea of Objects*, Sours (1980) describes anorexia nervosa as a flight from the controlling mother, and calls the anorectic's determination "a caricature of will." He writes: "The anorectic struggles against feeling enslaved, manipulated, and exploited. She believes that she has not been given a life of her own. . . . Her goal is power, expressed by a grand gesture which gets its energy from the fact that it is difficult to stop anyone from starving herself." A young woman told me, "I'd reject food to get power and to make her [the mother] fix it the way I wanted it."

The power of the anorectic is delusional insofar as it is dependent on a gross denial of reality, which may lead to death. The failure of reality-testing attests to the unreliability of the ego functions. The power comes from opposition, from the no-saying that is particularly characteristic of the second year of life. She not only says no to her mother; she also says no to the biological demands of her own body that are now felt to be as alien as were the demands of her mother. She focuses on being her idea of perfect and omnipotent so that she will need nothing and no one outside of her own self. When Sours says that the symptom is a caricature of will, he is recognizing that, as a child, the patient was derailed from the developmental continuum when intrinsic power—the "I am, I can, and I will"—should be consolidating.

The "no, I won't eat" or the "no, I won't go to the bathroom" may constitute the child's first statements defying parental power. She may not be able to control the parent, but may believe she can at least control what comes into or goes out of her own body. Freud ([1923] 1961) noted that the first ego is a body ego and could be regarded as "a mental projection of the surface of the body." The skin is where the baby can first differentiate inner from outer, from what is "inside me" to what is "outside me." The future anorectic protects the inner me from what is outside at the gates of the self, where what is outside can force its way inside.

When parents cannot tolerate acts or statements of self-determination and override them by force, the child is rendered totally powerless and is humiliated by this very impotence. Later in life, individuals who have had this experience in the early years will be likely to resist with all the power they have at hand what they feel to be the demands and intrusions made on them by others. What they experience as attempts to control them will elicit rage and active or passive resistance.

Working with the anorexia patient in psychotherapy, issues of identity, boundaries, and autonomy are spelled out, and the alliance is explicitly defined in a way that carries no threat of either loss of autonomy or abandonment.

Patient: I could starve to death and no one would notice.

Therapist: It's one way to find out if they care.

P: Yes, it is.

T: That puts you in a difficult bind—either it feels as though people are neglectful and don't care, or as though they are being intrusive.

P: It's not so much the intruding I resent. It's more the actual control, the presumption that what they say—when I get irritated and panicky if someone says I should eat. I don't like that. They should leave me alone and let me go the course I've set for myself.

T: That interferes with your autonomy.

P: Yes. Even if I can say no, just the fact that they think it.

T: When I said I wanted you to see Dr. L. to make sure you don't get sick, did that feel like I was interfering with your autonomy?

P: No. I felt guilty because I know you're right. You have the right to say that because you're looking after my psyche. If I had a more sure sense of myself, I wouldn't have to put on a label, a quantity, to everything. This identity thing is definitely true. If I can put good or bad labels on myself, it gives me a sense of who I am if I don't have the gut feeling.

And later in the session:

> **T:** It sounds like you fear that your wish for passivity will get the better of you.
>
> **P:** I have to struggle against it, to have to do things I don't want to do. I guess that's not really cracking up.
>
> **T:** I hear a protest: "I don't want to. Don't make me."
>
> **P:** I'm afraid I would be sucked into a vortex of helplessness. Tell me I won't.
>
> **T:** I don't think you will so long as we keep plugging away.
>
> **P:** That makes me feel better.
>
> **T:** You're not alone in your struggle. You do have a partner.
>
> **P:** But no one else is. If anyone else is my partner, they go away.
>
> **T:** Like I did last week?
>
> **P:** But you'll be back. I know you're there.

In this session, I emphasized the issue of the alliance, and by so doing also defined the situation as one in which she will not be abandoned. But I had to be careful to say that although I will "hold" you, I will do so in a way that will not overpower you. The use of "we" defines this aspect of the situation. At this point I gratified the need for a powerful object with a statement of reassurance (see the discussion of Myerson on page 96). I found that neutrality was sometimes experienced by her as an abandonment, which she could not work with therapeutically at this time. When I gratify the need here, I provide the holding environment she needs at this stage of vulnerability. Greenson (1970) writes:

> The most brilliant interpretations of unconscious meaning are valueless, even harmful, if the patient feels he is losing contact with his inner self and outer reality and desperately needs emotional and visual contact with me as a concrete, real, and predictable person. . . . I must become the bearer of reality, the emissary between reality and fantasy, for the patient. . . . I have to supply for my borderline patient what my neurotic patient does for himself.

Failure to intervene appropriately with respect to the patient's core relationship problem in the presence of significant failures of ego functions will set up a difficult character resistance. The above example illustrates how attention to the core issue and its resulting vulnerabilities enables the work to proceed.

While, theoretically, a therapist might make this core relationship problem an organizing principle for analytic therapy, there are instances when the life and death implications of the patient's acting out require treatment programs that entail combined medical, psychological, physical, and nutritional intervention. A good outcome would be more than an abatement of the anorexia itself; it would include the development of a reality-related self with emergence of intrinsic power and the capacity to have relatively normal relationships with others.

While bulimia and anorexia nervosa have been used to exemplify the concept of the symptom as a resistance, it is certainly not limited to these specific examples. Upon meeting a new patient for the first time, it will serve the therapist well to wonder how the presenting problem or symptom is the key to the illness and not the illness itself. With this in mind, he or she is far less likely to get embroiled in a collusive transference–countertransference resistance. It is always easier to prevent the setting up of an impasse than to extricate one's self and the patient from it later on.

BIPOLAR DISORDER

Mood disorders are so named because a disturbance in mood is the predominant feature—it is the main symptom. Just as a fever is a sign of illness and not the illness itself, these mood swings can be seen analogously as the temperature swings of the mind. What currently appears to have become a wastebasket diagnosis is that of bipolar disorder. Once the medical diagnosis has been made, a medical treatment is instituted. More and more, I hear this diagnosis applied when it is clear that the therapist is unable to understand the complexities of the patient's difficulties. In this instance, what we see is a countertransference resistance, a way to manage the difficult situation with the patient that makes the therapist feel better. At the same time, many psychiatrists are working hard to ensure that those working with the medical model include psychodynamic work as well. They agree that the simple and restrictive view of a medical model too readily invites therapists of all mental health disciplines to turn to narrow diagnostic formulations, medication, and organic explanations. They pay close attention to the transference–countertransference implications of prescribing a drug. Will the patient experience it as the therapist's wish not to be bothered with the patient's difficulties? What does it mean with respect to the core relationship problem? Or, on the other hand, does it shore up and enhance an important function of the ego that is necessary to do the psychodynamic work, but that is frail or absent because of early developmental derailment?

Affect as Part of the Character Structure

The therapist needs to ask: "What about the underlying character structure? What is the internal organization of self- and object representations and what is the affect that goes with each self and object set up in the unconscious?"

Depression is the affect that goes with loss of connection with the object, whether in actuality or in the mind, consciously or unconsciously. Freud (1926) describes a developmental sequence of dangers: first, that of object loss, then of loss of the love of the object, and finally, of the loss of the love of the superego. Loss of the love of the superego is like the loss of the love and approval of the object, who has been internalized and with whom there is now an identification in the form of the superego. In his paper on the "loving and beloved superego," Schafer (1960) notes that, in the hostile aspect of the superego, object hate is turned around and transformed into self-hate, while in the benign aspect of the superego, object love is turned around and transformed into self-love.

In normal, relatively healthy intimate relationships, an individual is likely to experience feeling "down" when an argument has caused a temporary breach in the relationship. Couples often report that their best sex is "making-up" sex, when the breach is healed. The intensity of the sex reflects the intensity of the joy at the reconnection. Elation or mania is experienced with the reconnection with the object, whether in reality or in the mind, consciously or unconsciously. Falling in love often activates the connection with the unconscious idealized self and idealized object. The mania may be the correlate with an activation of the grandiose self, which goes back to that stage of normal development (Mahler 1968) when the child still experiences mother's magical powers as his own.

The earlier the derailment from the developmental continuum, and the more severe the disruption of object relatedness, the more profound and pervasive an underlying depression will be—going all the way back to the anaclitic depression, the empty despair of the black hole. At the same time, pathological defenses against this depression are mentally constructed, including a persecutory connection with another, or the belief in the omnipotence of the self (a self who does not need anybody else), which accompanies manic states. While the defense of schizoid detachment may allow the individual to maintain a state of equilibrium that allows for functioning in the world that looks quite normal, the underlying depression is always close at hand.

In object relations terms, whatever its biological concomitants, a mood disorder is, at its very foundation, a relationship disorder. Going back to the earlier chapters of this book, we could add what the likely affective component of each situation would be. For example, power and pride evoke elatedness. Powerlessness and shame evoke depression. Underlying issues of power and pride vis-à-vis the parent comprise the relevant core relationship problem. The child's self-esteem will rise and fall with the esteem in which she is held by her mother. The mother who blocks intrinsic power blocks healthy pride as well.

  Depression in adolescence may be evoked when the developmental thrust of individuation stresses an underlying insecure attachment and a failure to achieve object constancy. When we hear of an alarming number of suicides in adolescents who have been given antidepressant drugs, perhaps it is not the effect of the drug itself that leads the boy or girl to such despair. Perhaps in being given a drug to make him or her feel better, the underlying insecurity with feelings of parental abandonment is exacerbated. They are not getting the psychological help they need, but which they can neither articulate nor request. They hear the message, "Don't bother us with your real pain." This is not unlike the situation when a patient has a negative reaction to the therapist's suggesting medication for her anxiety or depression. I have heard, "You just can't deal with my anxiety," or, "You don't want to know about my depression." And the patient is probably correct. Sometimes suggesting or prescribing an antidepressant is a manifestation of a countertransference resistance. And in this respect, the symptom of mood changes becomes the source of resistance.

  An interesting case of intransigent depression in therapy is that of a man who was raised by and close to a chronically depressed mother. In his wish to connect with her, he had no choice but to connect with her depression as well—that is, to join her by also being depressed. He certainly could not run in from school or from playing to tell her excitedly about the happy activities of his day. She would not connect with him, leaving him abandoned. With the loss of connection, he would experience his own depression. The symptom of depression signified both his connection with and loss of connection with his object. A therapy aimed at helping him get over his depression threatened his connection with her. He had a very negative reaction to the idea of medication. The therapist found herself to be depressed during and after his sessions. Any attempt to connect with him would lead to her being depressed, just as it happened with him and his mother. Furthermore, the therapist's sense of powerlessness evoked its own depression. Her wish to have him "fixed" by means of medication was a manifestation of her countertransference resistance—her wish to make the relationship more pleasant. His transference resistance was to what he saw as her obvious wish to have him get over his depression. He had to protect his inner connection with his mother.

  In a situation of dissociated self-states, each has its own self- and object connection that is also characterized by the affect specific to that connection. A self vis-à-vis the abandoning object is both angry and depressed. A self involved with a mother who can only be close to her child when he is able to deny his separateness may feel elated at the illusion of their restored oneness.

When a depression or mania is so severe as to interfere with the ability to function in the world, of course it is necessary to restore the individual to at least having the ability for self-care. Whether or not the individual will then be accessible to depth psychotherapy will depend on other findings in an overall evaluation. But if that capacity is there, turning to the question of developmental derailment and the underlying core relationship problem will be an important place to start such treatment.

In the next chapter, a verbatim report of a segment of brief therapy illustrates the importance of dealing with transference resistance.

13

Interpretation of Transference Resistance in Brief Psychotherapy

PRINCIPLES OF BRIEF THERAPY

The principles of brief therapy aim for the prevention of a therapeutic style that would prolong treatment (Horner 1995). Some of these principles are equally useful in long-term treatment, although their application would vary according to the therapist's sense as to what will be useful and appropriate with any given patient. Therapists who have trained in brief therapy have reported how much their long-term work improved by the judicious application of some of these principles. The principles for brief therapy are:

- activity
- clarity
- specificity
- immediacy
- interpreting upward
- maintaining the focus
- vigilant monitoring and interpretation of the transference, whether it be expressed directly or by allusion
- interpreting the triads

ACTIVITY

The therapist does not sit back and wait for the material to unfold. From the very beginning, he is active in the maintenance of the focus, in the interpretation of the transference, and in the application of the other mechanics essential to time-limited treatment.

As therapy moves from the uncovering phase to the working-through phase, the therapist will be less and less active, allowing the patient to take increasing responsibility in confronting his own defensive postures, such as passivity or vagueness. Indeed, by the end of the treatment, if all transference resistances are dissolved, the patient will take active responsibility for the scheduling of termination.

Clarity

The therapist should never assume he or she understands what the patient means if this meaning is not patently clear. Vagueness as a defense protects the patient from awareness of thoughts or feelings that would evoke anxiety. The defensive style itself is confronted with a simple statement such as, "You are being vague." This will most likely provoke some anxiety that may be connected with the therapist as a transference resistance, or that may be connected with the repressed material itself. Exploring the dynamics behind the resistance will be part of the therapeutic process.

Clarification is also indicated when the material presented is incomplete, being characterized by a narrative quality without the feelings or beliefs that were operative at the time of the event being reported. Inquiry about the missing elements of the experience is indicated to clarify what was actually going on at the time relevant to the therapeutic focus.

The use of words assumed to have consensual meaning when it is more likely that they have specific meaning for the patient should be clarified. Words like "rejection" in particular lend themselves to this kind of obfuscation. What does the word *signify* for the patient? (Horner 1995). What constitutes a rejection for this person? What is the fear? The fantasy? The reaction?

Indication of affect must be addressed, even though the patient communicated nonverbally, as with a smile. The inquiry into the feelings being experienced then leads to associations and memories that deepen the exploration and work of treatment. For example, the therapist may ask, "Are you aware you are smiling?" The patient may then report what the association was that evoked the smile.

Specificity

Global statements about the self, such as "I usually back down when someone disagrees with me," are unproductive and tend to be more ruminative than analytic. Asking for specific examples of times the person has backed down under such circumstances in his current life, such as at work or with parental figures, enables full exploration of the dynamic. Instances of the dynamic in the treatment situation should be noted and explored. The elucidation of the transference resistance is furthered by this exploration.

When the patient says things like, "I hide things," "I'm afraid of feelings," or "I think I've been self-destructive," the therapist may be fooled into thinking that the patient is dealing with important material when he makes such general statements. But they are probably things the patient has said about himself many times before without subjecting these statements to any kinds of exploration. Examples of this were given in chapter 10, which discusses common attitudes as resistance.

Vagueness and generalization may create the illusion that work is being done by the patient. However, in retrospect it is realized that very little of substance has been accomplished. As time is of the essence in brief psychotherapy, it is critical that nonproductive verbalizations are converted to become productive. This may be accomplished either by interpreting the vagueness and generalization as serving a defensive function, or by confronting it in a manner that blocks the patient from continuing in this mode, thus raising his anxiety level. An effective response can be evoked by means of systematic inquiry as to specific details that the patient is avoiding by vagueness or generalization.

IMMEDIACY

Attending to what is going on in the transference allows for the connection of thought, feeling, and impulse at the experiential level. The therapist should be alert to nonverbal signs that the patient is experiencing something he is not reporting. This should be attended to with inquiries such as, "What's going on?" or "What are you experiencing?"

INTERPRETING UPWARD

Patients selected for this form of brief therapy have been evaluated as being at the Oedipal level of development before treatment starts. The table of ego functions in chapter 2 was originally developed for purposes of such evaluation.

Inasmuch as there are bound to be perseverating pre-Oedipal issues with every Oedipal patient (unresolved orality in psychosexual terms, rapprochement issues in object relations terms, or narcissistic vulnerability in self-psychology terms) the therapist has to make a clinical decision when these issues emerge. They can be interpreted with the earlier developmental metapsychology as an organizing principle, such as is described in this book. But by interpreting downward, so to speak, the therapist encourages or facilitates a more regressive stance vis-à-vis the treatment process and transferentially. As regression is to be avoided in brief therapy, one interprets this same material within the context of the Oedipal triangle and its conflicts. A fear of maternal punishment by the withholding of maternal support or love is interpreted as a consequence of the competitive strivings vis-à-vis the father. The narcissistic wound of the Oedipal defeat is interpreted within the framework of the competitive evaluation of the self vis-à-vis the rival. If the patient is unable to work with this kind of material within the Oedipal framework, but seems traumatized by such interpretations, we have to assume he is not a candidate for this approach.

MAINTAINING THE FOCUS

The definition of a therapeutic focus at the start of brief treatment is part of the evaluation process—that is, determining whether or not it is possible to define the problem in terms of a specific conflict that can be uncovered and worked through in a relatively brief time period. The recognition of more complicated psychological situations may indicate that the individual is not suitable for this approach. The interpretation upward is an example of how the focus on the Oedipal focus is maintained, even in the presence of issues that can be otherwise conceptualized. If the problem is not focal, the patient is not a candidate for this approach to brief treatment. Other forms of brief treatment (Mann 1973, Malan 1976) may formulate other focal conflicts as their organizing principle—that is, issues such as loss. If the focus is not maintained, the therapist may find himself or herself on the road to more traditional long-term psychotherapy.

MONITORING AND INTERPRETATION OF THE TRANSFERENCE

Transference *reactions* are reactions primarily based on past relationships rather than on the reality of who the therapist is, or on the reality of the nature of the therapeutic relationships. These reactions are based on *current wishes or fears,* however, despite their origin in the past.

   Transference resistance—the focus of this book—refers to a manner of relating to the therapist that is intended, consciously or unconsciously, to make certain infantile wishes come true or to prevent what is feared from coming about. This way of relating, of managing the therapist and the therapy—*to bring about a predetermined outcome in the relationship*—will also be characteristic of the individual's manner of relating in other relationships about which he is in conflict.

An example of the therapist's collusion with this kind of resistance would be giving advice or answering the patient's questions in response to the patient's passivity and dependency. Interpreting the transference includes what the patient is doing and why he is doing it. The patient's reaction to the interpretation may elicit another transference reaction. This also needs to be attended to and explored. In brief therapy the therapist does not have the luxury of thinking, "This will come up again. I'll attend to it then."

The term "exploiting the transference" refers to the use of positive transferential feelings of the patient toward the therapist for the purpose of bringing about a therapeutic goal. Freud ([1917] 1957, 443) refers to the "unobjectionable positive transference." The therapeutic alliance depends to some degree on these positive feelings. Freud adds that we need not bother about it, as long as it operates in favor of the analytic work, but we must turn our attention to it when it becomes a resistance. The greater the degree of distortion of reality contained in these positive feelings, and the more they stand in opposition to thoughts, feelings, or impulses that would endanger them, the more they become a resistance and must be interpreted. A basic trust that is consistent with the present reality, although it is derived from the past, is currently adaptive and even necessary to the alliance.

Any actions or statements by the patient that only *allude* to the treatment situation should be explored in a here-and-now interpersonal focus, relating it to the therapeutic focus determined at the start of treatment to be the core issue. Examples of situations where this has become evident are lateness, the patient talking in generalities about her reaction to authority figures, bringing up old therapists, or complaining about doctors or about therapy in general. A patient may report a dream about going to the "eye doctor." Recognizing this as a transference dream about the "I doctor" (the therapist), the therapist will interpret it as such.

In the course of the interpretation of transference, a therapist should note if there is a passive compliance and agreement as contrasted to using the material actively in a working alliance. Transference reactions or postures may be subtle. Should the patient compliment the therapist on an astute observation, one has to look at how the patient feels about the therapist for making it. Behind the compliment may well hide competitive envy or resentment. We may say with some degree of certainty that when there is an impasse in treatment, long or brief, it is due to unanalyzed transference resistances that are acted out in the treatment situation.

THE TRIADS OF INTERPRETATION

The triad of conflict, anxiety, and defense is explored within the determined focus. For example, the anxiety and guilt associated with the conflict between the wish to love and the wish to compete with the parent of the same sex is defended against with a reaction formation in which the aggression is transformed to placating behavior and turned against the self.

The Oedipal focus is on the triangular situation with mother, father, and patient. Both legs of the triangle must be explored and then interrelated with respect to parents, as well as in the context of derivative triangles.

The focus is explored within the triad of past relationships, present-day relationships, and the transference. For example, the wish to be special to father, the wish to be special with the boss, and the wish to be special with the therapist are tied together dynamically. The presence of the same conflict, anxiety, and defense in each of these situations is explored.

CASE STUDY

The following material is from the brief treatment of a forty-year-old man who was employed in a highly responsible technical position in the communications industry. The presenting problem was his failure to advance in his work. A previous course of treatment with another therapist left the major transference resistance, his passivity and failure to challenge the authority of the therapist, untouched.

American-born, his newly arrived Oriental family had reestablished a clan-style of life, with the extended family living within a single household in which the oldest uncle was the undisputed leader of the family. The patient was the middle of three children.

It should be noted that in the evaluation interview, the patient reported an inability to recall the early relationships with his parents and he denied a significant emotional relationship in the present. Only one side of the triangle (the father side) was evident, and there only in terms of derivatives. Because he fit the diagnostic criteria and because he was highly motivated and interested in the brief approach, we made a decision to go ahead. The focus was defined as his fear of competing, of challenging authority, and of doing what he had to do to get ahead in his career.

What is interesting in this case is the emergence of the Oedipal issues and his readiness to look at them in the context of the focus initially agreed on. Although this is an atypical case, adherence to the principles of brief treatment led to a breaking through of the character resistances so that the early repressed material could emerge. The Oedipal situation was also atypical because it involved the uncle, although the mother–father–patient triangle also soon became evident. The wish to admire the father and to be special to him was as strong as the wish to be special to the mother. The uncle interfered on both counts, while the mother passively came between the children and their father.

The sessions reported here are predominantly from the uncovering phase of treatment, although in the seventeenth session we begin to see a shift to the working-through phase. It was only after a steady confrontation of character defenses that the underlying Oedipal issues began to emerge. Although the therapist was a woman, the transference was characterized by the patient's attitude toward the male authority figure, an amalgam of the feared uncle and the loved father.

Note especially the fast pacing and activity level of the therapist. This stands in sharp contrast to that of long-term treatment, in which the therapist does not want to interfere with the associational process.

SESSION 1

P: I've watched my colleagues pass me by. I'm pushed around by circumstances and by others. I don't like that either. I'm afraid to speak up and tell how I feel, and then I make excuses to myself. I don't show leadership to my kids either. My wife is in control by default. We get along well, but there is a leadership problem. I stay in the background, but would like to set an example to my kids. At work, I have a reputation for being a good worker, but I'm not the one to be in charge. Now I'm in a situation where I have to interact more and have to tell others what to do.

T: How is that for you?

(Inquiry aimed at moving away from intellectualization to experience.)

P: I feel defensive. I'm not used to telling people what to do. I don't feel superior to them, so I'm apologetic. I try to cover all grounds so I won't be attacked or criticized.

T: How does that work for you?

(Move to making the defenses less syntonic.)

P: I get cooperation. I bring the other side in so they're in it with me, so it's as much my problem as theirs. We're on equal footing. They accept my comments.

T: It sounds like it works, but you don't feel good about it.

P: We all want the same goal, but I don't like the feeling I have inside. People who were junior pass me over. Since I saw Dr. L. I realized the situation more. My unfortunate old habits are strong and I fall back. I don't retreat to a shell as much, but if I'm not on guard I fall back.

T: What was the impact of Dr. L.'s death for you?

(Exploring unresolved transference with previous therapist. The patient had not been in treatment for some time when Dr. L. died suddenly and unexpectedly.)

P: It was a big loss. I was sad. I thought he was selfish. He could have helped me and others.

T: You sound angry.

(Clarifying affect: tone of voice and posture.)

P: I'm disappointed. I recalled I liked him. I could communicate very well with him. It was a sudden loss, a disappointment.

T: And what was the effect of the disappointment on you?

P: I don't recall feeling any different. I saw him once a month. Before that, it was every week. After a year, it didn't have to be as frequent. I went back to recharge my batteries. It was the holiday season so I didn't see him that time. I felt sad and disappointed, but no other feeling.

T: You saw him as an energy source.

(The dynamic of the unresolved transference.)

P: I relied on him. It could be an area I was so used to as a kid. My parents took care of everything. I was protected and sheltered. That's where I get my attitude of dependency. It's more comfortable to have someone to depend on. That all came out with analyzing. I'm aware that I'm emotionally and psychologically dependent.

T: It sounds like the wish for someone strong to rely on is part of the overall pattern.

(Exploring motivation.)

P: That's an area he and I covered.

T: Was that your insight?

(Exploring motivation.)

P: There were two levels of understanding. The intellectual level was very reasonable. But the emotional level had no experience or exposure, so I don't know. I can rationalize or justify. I'm not used to the gut level. If I have a gut-level response, I will be passive. I take the path of least resistance. I try to please. I'm not sure of myself.

T: You had a reaction when I said I would not see you for what Dr. L. charged you and said my fee would be higher. What were those feelings?

(Responding to transference allusion of previous statement.)

P: I came prepared intellectually.

T: What do you mean?

(Asking for clarification.)

P: I'm embarrassed. I have no strong feelings.

T: Your embarrassment suggests you turn your negative feelings onto yourself.

(Exploring defensive style.)

P: That would be consistent with my behavior. At work and in general, when I make an assertion and someone doubts or questions me, I first react as though I did something wrong rather than say he doesn't know.

T: Can you give me an example?

(Asking for specifics.)

P: With my boss, Sam. I'd have an idea about a problem and the way I see what the priorities are. Then he'd come back and say the other way is better. Then I'd withdraw.

T: How did you feel toward Sam at that moment?

(Probe for feelings versus obsessive style.)

P: As we are talking, I am experiencing fear. Maybe I'm not being too accurate. When Sam comes back with a rebuttal, the only reaction I remember is annoyance. I don't know if there was fear then. Then I felt resignation—a "you're the boss" attitude.

T: You experienced fear as you told me about it.

P: On coming here, I felt it in my gut, like the first time with Dr. L. It gradually disappeared. The thought just occurred to me, when I first meet someone, I'm on guard. Then I get used to the situation. I bring it up because it relates to my dealing with my inner self. When I first met Dr. L. I tried to get to my inner feelings. But I drift back to my old self. Also with my boss. When I'm in a more assertive mood, I'd go in and interact with Sam in a different way and would get more favorable results, especially in the first few instances. But I'd drift back.

T: You said before that you resent him, then you withdraw and turn the negative feelings on yourself. Let's look at what starts the drift back.

(Exploring defensive style, which will be evident in resistance.)

P: I set a goal, like a pay raise. I prepare myself intellectually and justify it. Then I talk to Sam. Once it's done, it doesn't matter if the goal is accomplished or not. I relax. There's nothing to work on.

T: It's hard to hold on to your ambition.

(Clarifying motivation.)

P: To my goal.

T: You said you wanted to move ahead.

P: True. It did occur to me that if I set specific goals, I'd do better. That's curing the symptom. I could set ten goals.

T: You're talking about justifying a single act, as contrasted with dealing with your ambition and your aggression in general.

(Cutting through denial of aggression.)

P: Maybe that is the problem. I tend to drift back because I don't have what it takes to own my ambition and aggression.

T: It goes underground.

(Interpretation of defense.)

P: I'm not sure what my ambitions are. Maybe to be at the limit of my potential. That's easier said than done.

T: Something stands in the way.

P: Yes, but I don't know what.

T: Our time is almost up. What are your feelings about our session and about continuing?

P: You're very sharp.

T: How do you feel about that?

P: It's very exciting and interesting, the things you put out. I have a picture in my mind that Dr. L. and I painted together of my background. You pinpoint my ambition. I'm not at ease with it.

T: What are your feelings?

P: It could be beneficial. I don't think I can come every week.

(He avoids answering, but time is up.)

T: If we are to work in the brief format it will have to be every week, and it will be limited to forty sessions in all.

(Reestablishing the contract.)

P: After the forty weeks, would I be able to come back periodically as I did with Dr. L.?

T: No. Our job would be to figure out why it was necessary for you to do that. You said it was to recharge your batteries. That implies you continued to see him as the source of power. That's what we'll have to understand.

(The therapist clarifies the contract and the focus.)

SESSION 2

T: What was your reaction to our last session?

P: I appreciated it intellectually. It made me think. I'm aware I don't do my best. I'm too tired much of the time and don't want to be bothered.

T: You said it was fear and resentment with Sam.

(Cutting through the denial.)

P: That's correct. Maybe fear of rejection.

T: How does that feel?

P: It felt bad.

T: How do you feel toward the person who rejects you?

P: Resentment. I feel bad about myself and blame myself.

T: You turn the resentment anger onto yourself. But first you felt it toward Sam.

P: It might be meaningful if I cast it in another light. I was rejected by my parents and there was nothing I could do.

(Obsessive helplessness.)

T: Give me an example.

P: It was a pattern, the way I was brought up. If I was obedient and got good grades, I'd get a pat on the back. If I did anything out of line, like fight, they'd come down on me.

T: And do what?

P: It's a general expression.

T: You're staying away from a specific memory.

(Confronting the resistance.)

P: I don't remember my childhood.

T: Did they beat you?

P: They'd scold me.

T: What did they say?

P: That I shouldn't do that, and that so-and-so was better behaved.

T: Like who?

P: My cousins. It was a big family, and we all lived in the same house.

T: Which cousins?

P: I don't remember. They'd say the other kids are better.

T: How did that make you feel?

P: I may be making it up.

T: What are you experiencing right now?

P: Fear. It's overwhelming.

(This should have been explored in terms of the transference.)

T: Did they threaten you with punishment?

P: No. They'd say if you behave badly, you make us look bad to the other relatives. That was the theme.

T: And is there fear in that?

P: Yes. I'm not sure if I loved my parents. I respected them. I didn't want them to look bad.

T: How does that work with the other authority figures—not making them look bad? How did it work with Dr. L. and with Sam and with me?

P: I don't do anything. That's just a premise I work on.

T: What do you do to make Sam look bad?

P: It never occurs to me that what I do will make him look bad or good. I don't want to look bad in his eyes.

T: If you were smarter and knew better what to do, that would make him look bad to others.

(Moving toward the conflict.)

P: I don't want to tell people what to do. It means I look better than they are. It didn't occur to me in relation to Sam consciously.

T: To succeed you have to be better. You say that's a bad thing to do to someone.

P: It makes sense. I've been feeling fear for the last ten minutes.

T: Is it because of what I said?

P: Yes. This whole conversation makes me afraid.

T: What are your associations to it?

P: It rubs off to my boy. He's ten and a top student. My wife and I can't stand that he tries to be no different from the other kids. There's peer pressure. He purposely avoids standing out.

T: Like you.

P: Yes.

T: How do you feel toward your son for doing that?

P: I was mad. He is better. He doesn't have to hide it.

T: You want him to look better and make you look good.

P: I want him to feel good about himself. I don't expect any benefit from it.

T: So then why are you mad at him?

(Cutting through the denial.)

P: He had a chance to play the piano for our friends. I wanted him to play. He made excuses. He could show how good he is.

T: You're angry, not worried.

(Clarifying affect: nonverbal behavior.)

P: Maybe the fact that if he performed, I'd look good.

T: And you're angry that he didn't.

P: That makes sense.

T: Your wanting to look good sounds like it was a competitive situation.

P: I'm mad at myself about it.

(Therapist should have noted he turned his anger on himself here.)

T: There is a conflict if to look good makes someone else look bad.

P: That's not true. There are occasions I feel good about explaining things to others. This week there was a problem to be solved. I explained the situation and felt good. I was in control. That only happens when I have all the information. If I'm missing a piece, I don't have the guts to come out and say what I think. I qualify what I say. It's okay if the other doesn't know anything or if I know everything.

T: Where you are clearly superior.

P: Where I have the upper hand and there are no questions. When someone asks a question and I try to explain, I withdraw and crumble before I have time to think out an answer. I'm defensive although I know the answer.

T: Can you give me a specific example?

P: With Sam. Also the boss. Bosses reinforce the fear. Colleagues too, but not as much.

T: Like who?

P: Jack. He's more knowledgeable. I divide them into people I'm defensive with. The other group is easygoing, but I'm also defensive with them. But I do better.

T: It depends on how much power the other person has.

P: Yes, or they know more.

T: How do you feel toward someone who knows more?

P: Respect. If it's someone I've known for some time, I don't mind asking them a simple question. If I barely know them, I shy away, though I need the answer. The way I feel when I talk to someone who is more knowledgeable—the word is subversive? Is that the word?

T: You're also thinking the word subservient?

P: Yes.

T: Do you know what subversive means?

P: No lackey. Not challenging what they say. A "yes" man.

T: Subversive?

P: Spies. I mean subservient. There are two groups.

T: With one you enjoy being powerful and with the other you are subservient.

P: Yes. I enjoy being powerful.

T: So when someone is powerful over you, they have what you want. How does that make you feel?

P: I don't know.

T: Do you like them?

(Pushing through the denial.)

P: Not in particular. Sam. I don't care for him. Or Len.

T: What do you dislike about Len?

P: He's a stronger case. He manipulates people. He uses people to serve his own qualifications.

T: So how do you feel toward him?

P: I don't like him.

T: Does he make you angry?

P: No. I don't like that word. When I'm with him, I'm subservient.

T: The same process as with your parents?

P: I'm going to see why I'm mad at my kid in the same vein. Maybe I fool myself. I thought I was just worried about him.

T: Maybe it's both.

(Stating the ambivalence.)

P: Sam doesn't do the job of a manager. He isn't organized. It's harder to work for him.

T: And it's hard to challenge that.

P: There's nothing specific to challenge. He's even vaguer than I am. Len is a different bag.

T: You dislike him even more.

P: Definitely.

T: You said you were feeling fear when you first came in. Are you still?

P: Not as much. No matter how unpleasant a person may be, when I get to know them, I think I can get used to them.

(Transference allusion.)

T: And has that happened with me?

P: *(Laughing.)* Maybe.

T: You experience me as unpleasant.

P: Yes. Last time I did. (*Laughs.*) (*On the way out the door.*) How do you feel about me? That you detected hostility in me?

T: Let's talk about it next time.

SESSION 3

P: I'm uncomfortable talking to you. Usually I don't like people who come on strong. That's why I don't like Len. He's high-handed.

T: What do you do with that kind of person?

P: I don't like them. I don't do anything. If I disagree with him, if he makes a general comment of no consequence, I would ignore it. If it's something to do with my work, I'd be intimidated. I would go along with it.

T: If the person has more power than you, you're afraid to challenge him.

P: Yes. Also with Sam. Just because he's the boss, I withdraw. I don't even think clearly.

T: We've talked about how, in your background, to make the other look bad is a hostile thing to do.

P: Yes, it is.

T: Are you just being agreeable with me now?

P: We laid the framework last week. It makes sense.

T: With me as with Len, are you just being agreeable?

P: I don't like how things are. It's the way I behave, the way I react. Our relationship is different from me and Sam. Here it's different. I explore. I tend to challenge more.

(There is a good working alliance.)

T: Last time on the way out you were concerned about my reaction to detecting your hostility.

(Reminding him of negative transference.)

P: I was only looking at myself. I don't like people who come on strong. A thought occurred to me. It might be my anticipation that you would come on strong and I prepared myself with hostility to protect myself. Maybe it's just your style.

T: Are you saying you're afraid of retaliation?

P: Intellectually, I acknowledge that.

T: You wanted me to reassure you I wasn't mad.

P: Maybe. It's my behavior pattern, like my reaction to my parents.

T: There's a link between your aggression, power, and looking good.

(Clarifying dynamics.)

P: It's frustrating. I have the opportunity to advance, but I dare not. I'm afraid I'll fall on my face. There's fear in me. If I go too far out on a limb, someone might cut it.

T: Who is the somebody?

P: A colleague. People who are jealous.

T: A jealous colleague.

P: They would challenge my work.

T: What about your jealousy?

P: I don't like it.

T: How do you feel to those who are over you?

P: I don't like to be subservient at work. If it's someone in authority to me, I can't handle it.

T: Was there a specific situation this week?

(Cut through generalizations.)

P: Someone equal to Sam's boss asked me to look into a problem. Instead of feeling delight, a challenge, I was scared. I didn't show it. I thought, how can I make myself look good in his eyes rather than about doing the job.

T: Does this put you in competition with Sam?

P: No, but he goes on to a different project. If I'm aggressive and forceful enough I can take over his responsibilities . . . advancement. But I'm too scared. I don't want to. Edgar came to me to ask me some advice. He normally goes to Sam. I was more afraid rather than accepting a challenge.

T: What would happen if you were to succeed?

P: It would feel good.

T: Then what could the feeling scared be about?

P: What if I don't do a perfect job? I won't look good. I would be ashamed in front of my colleagues. I don't want that. A new woman has joined us. I've been in the department longer. She's the aggressive type and is taking more responsibility from Sam. I'm feeling left out.

T: You're in direct competition with her?

P: Yes, to compete for Sam's attention.

(A triangle.)

T: How about for his job?

(Should have stayed with the triangle and the competition he was acknowledging with inquiry about the parental triangle.)

P: I never thought about that.

T: Would you like his job?

P: I don't know.

T: But you said you like being in the powerful position.

P: I like having the knowledge.

T: But power is a core issue, as compared with being subservient.

P: If I know there is power.

T: Knowledge is just the vehicle to power. You are reacting to this woman moving into your territory.

P: We have our own territory. Our work is not in conflict. At one time it was and I didn't like it.

(Denial of present conflict.)

T: What were the circumstances?

P: I was responsible for the overall checking out the system. I'm the analyst. She's responsible for testing out the system. I didn't like working on it with her and thought I'd have to show that. I did it by being uncooperative.

T: You expressed your aggression passively.

P: Yes. Maybe she detected it. She probably talked to Sam and got herself off the project. I was in charge.

T: How did you feel about the situation?

P: Angry.

T: At whom?

P: Probably her.

T: How about the one who assigned her, who chose her over you?

(Looking for triangle issues.)

P: If I was angry at Sam, it wasn't obvious.

T: You don't let yourself know whom you are angry at. That is one defense you use.

(Confronting resistance.)

P: Yes. I use the technique of not knowing.

T: You use being ignorant as an aggressive act.

P: I do that a lot.

T: You also avoid conflict by being aggressive in passive ways.

P: That's correct.

T: How do you feel about that?

P: I don't know. It worked.

T: What do you mean?

P: She backed off.

T: Did you feel you had won?

P: No.

T: You avoided the issue and don't feel good about yourself.

P: Yes, I did avoid it. When I found out she backed out I wasn't especially happy. I was scared. Can I handle it myself?

T: So you use the defenses of being passive, of not knowing, of acting inadequate, and then you can't see yourself as up to the job.

P: That's right.

T: What are you experiencing right now?

(Patient appears upset.)

P: Fear.

T: How are you experiencing me?

P: You're pushing.

T: How do you feel about me for doing that?

P: Unfriendly.

T: Unfriendly?

P: I sense it. I don't feel hostile, but quite unfriendly.

T: What would you like to do?

P: I'm trying to find an answer. Darn it. You're right. I'm trying to find a way out. I'm looking for something to explain away and push aside the thrust of your observation. With that frame, I can't go anywhere. I don't know how my low self-esteem and my defense mechanisms go hand-in-hand.

(Working alliance.)

T: Do you feel I made you look bad?

P: Yes. I feel embarrassed.

T: I did something bad to you.

P: Yes, and I feel defensive and am trying to find a way out. What can I do?

T: Is being helpless a passive way to make me lay off?

P: That hits home. *(Short silence.)* It's easier to say I should be more positive. I fail in confrontations with my colleagues. I need time to think about what you said. Say it again. *(Passivity.)*

T: What?

P: How my reaction ties in with not wanting to look bad or not wanting Sam or Len to look bad. If I am more positive and challenging, I might make them look bad. So I fall back on my tricks?

T: How does that sound to you?

(Trying not to collude with the passivity.)

P: Logical.

T: What's missing is your fear of their reaction to your challenge, like what you felt toward me last session.

P: That makes sense. That's a lot to think about.

SESSION 4

P: The more I think about the conclusion, I'm too afraid to rub people the wrong way, to make them look bad. That's one of the major handicaps to my moving ahead. For example, my wife and I are aware of it. We bend over backward trying to be nice and not rub people the wrong way. How can I change my attitude? It's a habit. I react without thinking and that puts me in a subservient position and I can't get out of it. For example, one of my colleagues left to go to a different project. My car was behind his car. I debated whether I wanted to wave at him or not. I'm guessing I was concerned that he might not like me if I didn't wave.

T: How were you feeling toward him at that moment?

(Cutting through the obsessive style.)

P: Mixed. He's good and I'd like him on my project. But maybe I'm a little threatened.

T: The threat is the competition.

P: I have the premise that he's better than I am technically. The way he behaves. He says things with conviction.

T: How do you feel toward him?

P: Uneasy.

T: Uneasy?

P: When people come on strong and I don't like it. When you talk about technical facts you're either right or wrong. But I'm uneasy.

T: So the issue is coming on strong.

P: We were discussing Larry. If I decide someone is more knowledgeable, there's no problem listening.

T: But how do you feel to him about that?

P: I know he's good.

T: I ask the negative side and you go to the positive side. You said you felt threatened.

(Confronting denial.)

P: He may come in and take over things I'm doing. Then he'll look good in the eyes of the superiors. I won't look as good.

T: You act passive and he looks good.

P: I didn't do anything.

T: How did you feel to him then?

P: I tried to shut him off.

T: You didn't answer my question. You told me what you did.

P: You want to know how I felt?

T: Yes.

P: I shut off my emotions.

T: Are you doing that now?

P: I don't like him that much, but it would be nice if he could stay and help the project.

T: What are the negative feelings?

P: I don't like him too much.

T: What do you mean?

P: The times he comes on too strong.

T: Can you give me an example?

P: No. I don't like him at all. I act cold. I stop the conversation.

T: What would you like to do?

P: Now I'm feeling indoctrinated. I'd like to punch him in the nose.

T: You're saying that to please me?

P: Maybe. That's why I used the word "indoctrinated." I keep quiet and act cool.

T: You use a passive way to express your anger.

P: I think so. But he picked up on it. Lately he's been acting in a more passive manner.

T: How do you feel about how he is now?

P: He's okay.

T: You dealt with the problem in a passive manner.

P: It's a habit I don't like. I don't know what to do about it.

T: You're being passive and helpless with me now.

(Interpreting the resistance.)

P: *(Laughs.)* I want to do something about it.

T: Like what?

P: I don't know. I can say something more. My wife is very sensitive. If people rub her the wrong way, she fights back and tells them she doesn't like it. She comes on too strong.

T: To you?

P: She used to, but not recently. Five years ago, when she did that I felt the same way. I resented it and then I withdrew. Now she's mellow. I bring this as evidence of what I don't want to be.

T: You seem to equate getting ahead as an aggressive act.

P: Other colleagues are more aggressive and assertive and they got ahead. I tell myself I want to be assertive.

T: But the more angry you are, the more you retreat.

P: Yes. I thought that if I really want to express a point that would hurt the other or rub him the wrong way. I have to work myself up so I can be assertive or say something unpleasant to the other person. I don't like it. It drains me. I don't want to be always on guard and prepared. What do I want to do?

T: You said you wanted to get ahead. That seems clear.

P: Yes. Now I'm confused.

T: When did you get confused?

P: When you said that about moving ahead.

T: Do you know how?

(Should have inquired how that statement created anxiety.)

P: Not by punching in the nose.

T: Is that what you feel like doing?

P: Yes.

T: So you know you feel resentful, but you smooth it over.

P: I could just tell them I don't like how they behave. That would be offensive.

T: What would happen then?

P: I'd take the other by surprise.

T: You'd hope they'd back down?

P: It's a dilemma. What if they're right? I don't want him to back down.

T: You said you would be offensive. How do you imagine he'd respond?

P: He might come back and be harsh. Maybe the thing to do is to stay calm and talk about the issue and leave emotions out of it. I seem to be drifting.

T: What are you experiencing?

P: Fear.

T: Toward me?

P: I'm not sure. I feel confusion.

T: The confusion acts like a smoke screen.

P: A mask. If someone comes on strong to me, the only thing to say is that he is too strong and let's calm down and talk about the issue. It depends on the circumstances.

(This probably refers to the transference.)

T: Give me an example.

P: Larry. I'd tell him let's calmly sit down and talk about it. Instead, I shut him off. I can't think of a social situation.

T: How about your wife?

P: I've conditioned her.

T: You said you had the same problem in the family.

P: Yes. I don't speak up. I can't recall an incident right now. A friend of ours told us she'd take care of something and backed down. I didn't say anything.

T: How did you feel toward her?

P: I would have liked to have said, "You said you would!" But I didn't. I hate myself for being that way.

T: You turn the anger on yourself.

P: Yes. I'm always like that. I try to say it in a vague way, and then I hate myself for not spelling it out.

(On the way out.) Is there a clue?

(Retreat to passivity.)

SESSION 5

P: I want to continue about Larry. He called me today and asked if he could come back to our project. Maybe I don't want it because I fear the competition. Before I wanted him to come back because I needed someone to lean on. I think I can deal with people I know better than with a stranger. My feelings about having him back are he's someone I need to lean on technically. But he might compete with me. Since I feel good about myself because I just had a few days off, I'm leaning toward forgetting about it. I don't feel so strong about having someone to lean on any more. That's a change from the feeling we talked about. I was thinking I might have reasons for why when the going gets rough I turn it back on myself. It has to do with my parents. They wanted me to do things the same way. Since I didn't, when I ran into a roadblock, the only way I could get their attention was to act in meek self-pity, so they would give me sympathy and notice me. If I fought them I'd only get a scolding.

(He begins to look at his defensive style.)

T: There was gratification in it even if it didn't feel very good.

P: It occurs to me that it fits the picture. That's one thing about psychology—you can twist things.

T: Are you twisting things when you say it fits?

P: I don't know how much it is because I am biased.

T: Do you think I may know better?

P: No. No one knows better than I do because I am who I am, but I think I could be influenced. I try to make things fit the premise. It fits my behavior. I try to mold into a prominent personality or event.

T: And that's going on with me?

P: It could be.

T: Let's look at that.

P: It also fits. I tend to mold myself into the environment. I don't stand up and be different. I don't know. It's too easy to twist things.

T: Are you twisting to fit in with me?

P: Yes. To fit the premise we are building. I turn it back to myself rather than be aggressive and try to change the dominating factor.

T: Is there something you disagree with me about but haven't said? You give me a lot of power.

P: Yes. I do. Also with my colleagues. I don't like that I give myself up before a confrontation or interaction starts.

T: Then how do you feel toward that person?

P: Subversive. I mean subservient.

T: That's the same error you made before.

P: But I also want to knock you down and be the one who is one better.

T: So that's why you said subversive.

P: It fits.

T: You have wishes to knock me down.

P: Yes. I don't like to be bossed around. I feel helpless. I give you total authority and don't even struggle. I don't like it. I can link that to my parents.

T: You had a wish to knock them down?

P: It's too far back. The only emotion I have now is I have to oblige them grudgingly.

T: Grudgingly?

P: I feel disgusted with myself. I feel helpless because I couldn't do anything about it. They were my parents. They knew better.

T: Do you have a reaction to what you just said?

P: No. The only thing I felt was that I was forceful when I put myself in their shoes, but I don't feel my own feelings. I erase myself. That's the pattern.

T: You felt their power, but not your own.

P: Yes.

T: To be powerful would be to knock them down, like here with me.

P: Not physically. But to gain the upper hand. At work today, I was able to speak more confidently. I felt I had the upper hand. I can only handle things at two levels—either I have the upper hand and am in complete control, or it's the other way around. I don't know how to be in between.

T: That seems to be the issue here.

P: And I do things to please you.

T: You make sure I don't feel threatened by you.

P: That's right. *(Sighs.)*

T: What are you experiencing right now?

P: Speaking about threatening—it occurred to me this week when I was driving to work, I asked myself if we were trying to find out the underlying things in me. I wonder and thought I should ask if I am getting anywhere. Am I getting my money's worth?

T: You're giving me the power to answer that.

P: This question would be aggressive to ask.

T: The form of the question is a subservient way to communicate.

P: That's true. It would take guts even to ask. Then I'm subservient.

T: What are the feelings and statement behind the question?

P: I'm looking for a prescription. When we know the problem there must be a prescription.

T: And I know it.

P: Yes.

T: That's what you did with Dr. L. You kept him knowing the answer and had to keep coming back to have your batteries recharged.

(The unresolved transference.)

P: I liked him, but I think you're right. I kept coming back for the prescription.

T: You kept yourself subservient to him and gave him all the power.

(Transference resistance.)

P: Is that true? It's a good time to try to merge the two things together. Dr. L. said that because of my parents' behavior to me, the premise was set up so that I am inadequate, and that's the premise for all my behavior. I was brainwashed. It's consistent if I try to act and not rub them the wrong way that I become inadequate.

T: Your feelings of inadequacy are related to your passive defenses against your own impulses and wishes.

(Upward interpretation of narcissistic issues.)

P: It's true I needed Dr. L. to recharge. I drift back and need someone to shake me.

T: How come?

P: I'm used to it.

T: There's a point at which you don't like it and have to push your feelings away.

P: You say I have feelings or impulses to knock down and not be subservient.

(The projection should be noted.)

T: What are you doing now?

P: I'm confused.

T: You got confused when I took the upper hand.

P: And you put me on the defensive. When the other gets the upper hand I ask questions instead of confronting. Back to my question. I can explain everything. So what?

T: You are being helpless.

P: I see. *(Laughs.)* You're really throwing it back at me.

T: How does that make you feel?

P: I was feeling scared. There's something in that. Maybe I try to do things on an intellectual level and suppress my emotions. What does it mean? Maybe the intellectual garbage is an escape. I don't let my emotions show. It just occurred to me. I tie it in with my parents. When I felt bad or tried to knock them down, I suppressed it. I had to explain it away. They were my parents and I had to be respectful. I couldn't handle my emotions. Having to let my emotions show is one of the answers.

T: How does that thought make you feel?

P: A little scared.

T: What's the danger?

P: If I ask you something, I take a risk. I may annoy you or rub you the wrong way. That's probably it.

T: Then what would happen?

P: I don't know. Now I feel like I'm acting to get sympathy. I was going to say I'm afraid you'll come back with bigger vengeance.

T: Then what?

P: I could fight back.

T: What would you do?

P: In a personal situation, if I know I'm right, I would try to do it in a mild manner.

T: How would you fight back in a mild manner?

P: I would hold on to my principles or ideas. I'd tell you as often as it takes. I'm thinking too far ahead. There's no end to it—two people talking to the wall. It wouldn't get the work done. I might bring in a new point, but if we were just emotional, we'd shout at each other.

T: How does that feel?

P: Scary.

T: What's the danger?

P: We'd come to blows.

T: What would happen?

P: I'd be knocked down or hurt.

T: Then what would you do?

P: I would keep fighting in my fantasy.

T: How do you feel about it?

P: They're just words.

T: How would you feel if you were knocked down?

P: I might kick or scream.

T: Where would you kick the person?

(This should have been related to the transference.)

P: Where it hurts. Where I could reach him. In my fantasy, I would fight with whatever power I could.

T: How do you feel about your fantasy?

P: Nothing. Not even fear. Before, there was fear.

T: Before you thought about fighting back?

P: Yes. But nothing now.

T: Do you feel good about it?

P: No. Now the fear is back. It isn't good and it isn't bad. It's a territory I've never been in.

T: But you fear it in your mind.

P: Even in this fantasy, I couldn't shake myself free from reality. I'm trying to placate you again, but there is the constraint of reality. He might be bigger. I might get hurt.

T: You're still staying away from feeling.

P: I have the idea now that I am trying to placate you.

(He begins to confront his transference resistance on his own.)

SESSION 8

P: I had a direct conflict with Sam. I knew what was happening all along. I couldn't say the proper words.

T: What were the exact circumstances?

(Asking for specifics.)

P: There was a meeting with Sam and his bosses. A point was brought up by the people who are helping me with the project. They presented a list of things still to be done, both large and small things. Sam's bosses asked questions and dwelt on it. I sensed something wasn't right. After the meeting, Sam asked me to get the solution to one of the points. The next day I talked with him and he blew up. He said it was a trivial point and he didn't want his bosses to waste time, as though we couldn't solve such a trivial problem. It makes us look bad. I was mad too.

T: About what?

(Asking for clarification.)

P: He seemed to blame me. It's not fair to blame me for that. I was also mad this morning because at the meeting, it seemed like the people who helped me stole the limelight. They got the credit for my ideas. I didn't come out. I could have put it in the right perspective, given my ideas. But I didn't. It didn't occur to me, but I knew I was mad and that they were getting the glory. The next day, I was mad that Sam was mad at me. I told him it was because we didn't want anything to fall between the cracks. He said we looked bad because it was trivial. I said it was a complete list and that we hadn't gotten around to doing it because it was low priority. I was mad at the people and at Sam.

T: Did you tell Sam you were mad?

P: No. But I think he knew. His voice cracked and his face was red. Normally, there's nothing I could do to Sam.

T: Like what?

P: Rebut him.

T: How do you feel about it right now?

P: More mad than anything else. Later, I talked to my colleague and he said if Sam's bosses were interested, that's just the way it is. It hit me, that's what I should have told Sam. But I was blank. Now I see Sam's problem. If I came up with a cold rational statement, I would shut him off. You sense in me that I want to knock him down in one punch. I didn't pick the right punch. I ended up doing what he told me to do.

T: You used the word "rebuttal." You said you were angry but your words were defensive.

P: An offensive stance didn't occur to me.

T: The feelings are angry; the words are placating and self-justifying. You changed being active to being passive.

P: I defended myself.

T: You did not challenge him.

(The passive stance toward the authority figure.)

P: That's true. It didn't occur to me to say what my colleague said.

T: It didn't occur to you to challenge him, but just to placate him?

P: I defended myself. What else can I do?

T: You are being passive with me.

P: And you say what do I want to do. It doesn't even trigger anything in my head.

T: You are automatically self-defensive and passive.

P: I was in the meeting, too, with the people who helped me and got the credit. I'm mad at them, but I didn't challenge them.

T: What stops you?

P: Myself. That's being vague.

(He catches his resistance.)

T: Yes.

P: The fear I may displease the other party. They might come back and punish me or give me a hard time.

T: What would you do then?

P: As I am, retreat. As I would like to be, fight back. But then, maybe that's just the indoctrination.

T: *(Shrugs.)*

P: Deep down I want to fight back or I wouldn't be seeking help here. I shy away from the challenge. I'm insecure.

T: You retreat from aggression. You turn to defensive passivity.

P: The fact I realized I'm afraid to challenge because the other might give me a hard time doesn't erase or overcome it, but the realization is a first step. The next time maybe I'll realize I have an option or alternative versus backing down and turning it on myself. That's the bottom line. Then it's up to me; I'd have a choice or option to make rather than just react. Act rather than react.

(A shift toward readiness to working through.)

T: How do you feel right now?

P: I feel good. It's something concrete to work on. It bugs me when things are vague and there's no specific direction. I feel good. Also scared. Something new just occurred to me. It just occurred that what I'm saying is nothing new to the extent that Dr. L. said the same thing. This is a different version. He said I have the option to take action on the old premise of an inadequate me or a new premise that I feel good about myself. You said something about accepting the challenge. That's more specific. I did use Dr. L. as a crutch. What's the difference now?

(The competitive motivation was missed in his previous treatment.)

T: What is it?

P: Now I say it out loud in a conscious manner. Before, subconsciously I knew I'd have to recharge.

T: In your relationship with him, you got permission to challenge. But even now you don't own your own aggression. You attribute it to my "indoctrination."

P: That is the point. Now I'm thinking what it means to own it. I probe the consequences. If I'm responsible for my own act or say it was someone else's idea. I just blanked out.

(Indicating resistance.)

T: What are you experiencing?

P: Scared. I'm scared.

T: Because you can't back down and say, "Don't be mad at me. It was Dr. L.'s idea or Dr. Horner's idea or my wife told me to do it."

P: That's right. That's one point that didn't hit me. I don't know what to say. It is the point. *(Silence.)* I'm thinking that it's true. At home, I hide behind my wife. At work, I hide behind whoever is convenient. When I ask someone else to do a certain task, instead of saying I want him to do it, I use Sam's name or the name of some higher authority.

T: Mhm.

P: Why would I not want to own that it's my idea or action? If I did, I would sound more aggressive. I'd rub someone the wrong way.

T: *(Shrugs.)*

P: Is there a connection between that and the fear of challenge?

T: When you ask me questions, you back down from a subtle challenge of my authority.

(Interpreting passivity as transference resistance.)

P: That's true. I can think of that scenario with my parents. The times I challenged them and they'd come back hard on me. To alleviate the situation, I'd disown the idea or the alternative of challenging them. It makes sense. They'd always negate whatever idea I had to challenge them. If I did challenge them, I'd say it was someone else's idea to smooth over the situation.

T: How do you feel toward them about having to do that?

P: I hate it!!

(The first expression of strong affect.)

T: You must hate it with me, too.

P: *(Sighs.)* Not yet.

T: You assume the defensive posture with me by asking questions.

P: That's true. But I'm confused. *(Laughs.)* Confused. I treat this situation like you are the teacher and I'm going to school.

T: And you never challenged your teachers.

P: For sure. It was an extension of my attitude to my parents.

T: You keep yourself dumb and the teacher and me smart and knowing everything. That's a placating stance.

P: It definitely is, and at times I knew I was doing it on purpose to make the other party feel good, to placate, and I don't like it. *(Sighs.)* I don't like it at all! *(Silence.) (Laughs.)*

T: What's going on?

P: I just have to go out and fight. That was a cynical laugh. Maybe self-pity. Why didn't I do that? *(Silence.) (Sighs.)* Another thing that's interrelated. A lot of times challenging is not a way to get something done in the project. You have to coax the other, to get them to do something for you to get the job done. But it doesn't conflict with the concept of challenge. You have to know what you're doing, if that's the way to get the job done. It has nothing to do with challenging. It all makes sense. But it is easier said than done.

(Working alliance.)

T: There's always the alternative—don't do it and continue to feel the way you feel.

P: That would be chicken. And I don't like it. Subconsciously, I haven't shaken my own program, the way I do things, but I do not like it!

SESSION 14

P: How have I been doing? I'm the one to answer that.

T: How come you asked me?

P: Maybe I experienced the need to recharge. I'm not making a lot of progress in owning my own actions.

T: Last session, we were starting to touch on family issues. Do you think you might want to pull away from that subject?

P: I don't know. I want a better feeling of how we stand. It's not going to be open-ended.

T: That's right. We agreed to a forty-session maximum. This is number fourteen.

P: It's time we should see if we're going in the right direction.

T: Do you have any thoughts about this?

P: No. The first few sessions we were uncovering new material. Now it's stagnant.

T: What seems to be missing?

P: We're not moving.

T: What was your reaction to our last session?

P: No reaction. I always said there is a stretch of ten to twelve years that I don't remember of early childhood. I suppress it. It must have some bearing.

T: What do you remember of the last session?

P: The fact that I couldn't deal with my uncle and hoped that my father would stand up to him for me. But he didn't. He let me down. The consequence is my habit of hiding behind someone I've put on a pedestal.

T: You've cut yourself off from your feelings about this. Maybe that's the piece that's missing.

P: I cut myself off because it's painful.

T: What are you experiencing right now?

P: I'm trying to reconstruct it. I recollect other clues of childhood.

T: Who was the dominant one, of your mother and father?

P: My mother. She was with us most of the time.

T: How was that?

P: I was closer to my brother and sister than to them. My sister was three years older and my brother was three years younger.

T: Who took care of you?

P: My sister was on her own with her friends. My mother always complained to us that my aunt and uncle gave her a hard time. She asked us to study to make her look good.

T: How did you feel about that?

P: The feeling was I had to try to protect her and take care of her. That was the dominant feeling, not love.

T: What's the difference between feeling loving and protecting?

P: It was different in our family. We never showed feelings. With my mother and father, it was business as usual. We all had a part to play.

T: You said you wanted to protect your mother.

P: Yes.

T: It sounds like there were feelings there.

P: I felt she was stepped on, and she couldn't defend herself.

T: Who stepped on her?

P: My uncle.

T: How did you feel toward him for stepping on your mother?

P: Mad. I hated him. It was all I could do—hate. I couldn't do anything. At times, I'd blow up and dispute him. I'd say something to his face, and then my mother would be the first to come down on me. It wasn't proper. It would incur more punishment on her. They'd say she didn't raise us properly to respect him and all that crap.

T: You felt loving and protecting to your mother, but you didn't get any loving appreciation back?

P: That's true.

T: How does that feel—to try to protect her and not to be rewarded with her love?

P: Betrayed! I stand up for you and you let me down! Betrayed. She might have explained afterward and I might or might not have understood, but the immediate feeling was that I was betrayed. After awhile, I closed my eyes and ears and said the hell with it.

(Strong affect.)

T: It sounds like there was a wish to be specially loved by your mother.

P: I think so. By comparison, my father lacks feeling, though mother plays her part. I interacted with her more, and feelings developed more with her. My father was away at work. I didn't see him much. There wasn't any communication.

(The wish to be preferred by father over his brother came out in an earlier session.)

T: Did your mother complain to you about your father?

P: No. The complication was that although I had love for my mother, because of her lack of love for my father, she was always nagging. We were the only ones she could hold on to as hers. It was the negative component of my feelings to her. In my relationship with her now, she tells me to take care of myself and the kids, nagging. I act like them to my kids.

T: You want your son to make you look good the same way.

P: Yes.

T: So there was a triangle with you and your mother and your uncle. You wanted to be special to her, but he'd win out and be more important to her.

P: I see. And my father was always on my uncle's side. There was no one to turn to. That's why I gave up.

T: You couldn't challenge your uncle's power and get specially loved by your mother for it, and you were mad at your father for not helping against your uncle.

P: Yes. I'm trying to think how this ties in with how I am now. It's obvious. I did try to challenge the authority, but I got back doom. In the family, everyone put me down, including the ones I hoped would back me up. Now it's a habit not to challenge. I expect the consequence of failure.

T: Last time you were saying how you did challenge Sam and won, but you didn't like that either, because then you couldn't keep him on a pedestal. You want him to be strong to stand up for you.

P: In the same context, I talked with Betty. She was saying how she'd do things and I disagreed. She said she has eighteen years of experience. I didn't say anything.

T: How did you feel?

P: I thought, baloney! So what! I still believed what I said.

T: She's like the uncle who can't be challenged?

P: Yes. That's a good point. Someone else came and she turned to talk to him. I didn't feel too bad about that. It did bother me a little bit.

T: A little bit?

P: It bothered me.

T: You turned it on yourself, then you made it small, like you had to respect your elders.

P: I don't have to be bothered.

T: You push it away as you did in your family. It's obvious you are bothered.

(Cutting through the denial.)

P: I am bothered by it.

T: Let's take a look at that.

P: The reason I am bothered is I believe what I said and then I was challenged by the authority.

T: You were diminished, as a child. She has eighteen years of experience.

P: Now I'm feeling scared.

T: What's that about?

P: Fear.

T: What comes to mind?

P: Nothing. I'm blank.

T: Are you feeling fear toward me?

P: No. If anything, I'd like to get the fear out and talk with you.

T: You weren't afraid of Betty but you were of your uncle. How do you feel to the one who makes you feel afraid?

P: I don't like it.

T: That sounds angry. As I push you, you get frightened.

P: Yes.

T: Maybe you are afraid of your own anger.

P: I don't remember where I expressed anger and didn't get bad consequences.

T: You got mother's betrayal.

P: That's right. It's interesting. I still don't want to own it.

T: Betrayal is a harsh word.

P: Yes, that's how I felt.

T: Can you connect now with how that betrayal felt?

P: No. All I feel now is fear. Scared. In here (*pointing to his chest*). I feel empty. A numbness.

T: Maybe the emptiness is the loss of your mother's love. You started by trying to be specially loved by her and then you lost that love.

P: Yes. I don't know what to think.

T: What are you feeling?

P: The same, but not as much. I hear what you said and I understand it.

T: Does that make you sad?

P: I feel lost. Maybe that's also a defense mechanism. I don't feel sad. That confuses the issue. I feel lost and I want someone to help.

(These are undoubtedly pre-Oedipal issues. For that reason, they are not picked up.)

T: Mhm.

P: I have an interesting blank in my head. (*Silence.*) I can tell myself that if I challenge the authority now, nothing will happen to my mother. Betty has influence on Sam, and I don't want to rub her the wrong way. I don't like her as a person. She's too domineering.

T: That's what you said about your mother.

P: That's true. In a way, my wife could also be called domineering, hot-headed. She does things her way. I'm probably more attached to people who dominate than not.

T: And you have to find a way to be special to that person. With your wife, you are protective with her about her work. You play out the same theme at work, wanting to be special and afraid to challenge.

P: I don't want to be a slave to the past.

SESSION 16

P: I ran into Sam this morning. He had to cancel a meeting because he had to take his car in for repair. I asked him if he needed a ride. On the way back, I didn't say much. Then I said I'd take him back to pick up his car. I'm so ready to offer help. I don't know if it's just a habit of trying to please, or am I playing politics?

T: We've talked about your wish to be special to your father over your brother and to be special to your mother over your uncle. Is there a wish to be special to Sam?

P: There definitely is. I want to be special with the boss.

T: It seems to have the same emotional meaning as being special to your mother and father.

P: Yes. I want to know what I'm doing and why. If I don't think about it, the chances are I'll act on the old stuff. I want to catch it before I react. I want to act, not react.

T: The wish to be special leads to placating behavior, though you wonder if it's political.

P: I always have a placating attitude. Speaking of that, a lot of times I tend to find a reason why I should want to, why I should be obligated to. I look for something in which he did me a favor and I am obligated.

T: Obligated to be nice?

P: Like the time our friend got us that special deal.

T: Do you think you may project that if you do someone a favor then you expect to be treated nicely—to be specially loved?

(Connection to the wish to be special to his mother for doing her a favor, that is, standing up to the uncle, should have been made.)

P: What's wrong with that?

T: You said it was a problem.

(Confronting the denial.)

P: I try to find the good intention no matter how evil the person is. I look for the shred of goodness and try to protect it. I justify why they do that.

T: What could be behind that?

P: It dictates how I behave. My concern is whether I do it because of my good nature or for political reasons. I look for the good intention in the other.

T: How about your parents?

P: That's what I was thinking, that I try to deceive myself. I don't want to think that my parents could ignore me and not appreciate what I've done for them. I try to justify for them and make excuses.

T: How would you feel if you didn't make excuses for them?

P: Rejected.

T: How do you feel to someone who rejects you?

P: Angry. Mad. I wanted to love my parents. I don't want them to admit that they rejected me, so I justify them.

(Defense against ambivalence.)

T: You explained away what they did to make you angry.

P: Right. *(Silence.)* That makes sense.

T: What are you experiencing?

P: A little scared. An empty feeling. I'm not sure if "empty" is the right word. It's congested. Tight.

T: Do you feel like crying?

P: Not so much. It's more fear. I don't cry when I'm scared. I do when I'm sad.

T: A minute ago when you said you felt congested, you hit your hand with your fist.

P: I did? *(Silence.)*

T: Does feeling scared have to do with your anger?

P: I'm back to feeling scared because I'm afraid that my anger could be very destructive. I'm not sure I understand this. The destructiveness. People won't love me any more. It's all a house of cards. Being a nice guy and being well loved—it would all collapse. *(Sighs.)* I don't know what to say.

T: What are you experiencing?

P: An emptiness in my head.

(Again, the pre-Oedipal issues are not picked up. Interpretation is upward.)

T: How does all this relate to what you were saying about Sam?

(Returning to the focal conflict.)

P: I said earlier that I want to see whether I did that for political reasons or because of the habit of being "Mr. Nice Guy." I want to be Mr. Nice Guy because I try to get the shred of goodness from anyone. It's my reaction to my parents' reaction. It's the same with Sam. I did say Betty is now his favorite. Because of that, I feel competitive to get his attention. It is possible this may be a consequence of that. I feel Sam rejects me. I'm confused. So I want to please him to get his attention. I show him the shred of goodness in me so I can be of use to him.

T: Emotionally, it's like competing with your uncle for your mother and with your brother for your father.

P: It's a no-win situation. I would have made the offer even if Betty were not in the picture. It's a habit to do something to please my parents because I felt their rejection when I stood up for them. Other times, I show I can be a nice boy and of use for them. With Sam, it's the same reason even if Betty were not there. The ultimate goal is the same. To show the shred of goodness and usefulness in me to the authority figure. The bottom line is I have to convince myself I'm good just by standing on my own feet.

T: That one can do by doing a job well. You make it a personal issue with emotional meaning.

P: That's right. You say I mix something personal in the work environment.

T: Yes. That's why there is so much uncertainty and anxiety about it.

(Interpreting transference issues in the work context.)

P: This time I want to look into it. I must be anxious or I would not have brought it up. In a sense, I don't even care if Sam likes me. Before, when we drove together, I'd initiate conversation and make it pleasant. Now I don't care. I was cryptic. I just discussed work or professional things. That's an improvement. But there's still the same anxiety. That reminds me. We were on the topic of my wife last time.

T: How do the things we are talking about now apply there?

P: Sometimes she does things to irritate me a lot because of her sloppiness. The kids take after her. I'm mad about it. I used to pick up for her, but I gave up.

T: Is that all you did?

P: No. I told her the place was like a pigpen. She joked about it. Sometimes she picks up and sometimes she doesn't. She complains there's too much to do. She hides behind that and says there are more important things.

T: What does sloppiness mean to you?

(Clarification of "sloppiness" as a signifier.)

P: *(Laughs.)* I could tie it to this fact. One way I tried to please my mother was to be tidy. She liked things tidy, everything in its place. It's something I still follow because I wanted to please her.

T: The wish to please her and to be special is very strong.

P: It seems to be. I wasn't aware of that. I can explain many things in that context. I'm also thinking about wanting my kids to be good in school. I wanted a reflection from them.

T: To look good.

P: Yes, but I wonder if it can't be explained because I wanted to please my mother.

T: If you look good, it pleases her because then she looks good.

P: It's so strong. I just want to be myself.

T: First you have to be aware of the unconscious factors that direct what you do. The wish to please your mother is very powerful.

P: It sure is. It sure is. And it's scary too.

SESSION 17

P: Last time, I realized what a tremendous influence my mother still has on me. It's related to my inhibition in challenging an authority. When I did, what I got back was an unpleasant experience. I got a twisted way of looking at the experience and tried to explain away my mother's behavior. We were talking about incidents when I was mad at my wife. She usually goes to sleep with the TV on. The other day, she was in bed and I went in and turned it on. She was mad and said I disturbed her sleep. I was really mad. I turned it off and left the room. I thought, how could I know, especially when it's her habit to leave it on? I went into the study and said, "Damn it!" I don't know if she heard me, but later, when I went back to our room, she apologized. She knew she had been unreasonable. That kind of thing happens a lot. She blows up and jumps to conclusions. Sometimes she's right and sometimes she's wrong, but I've always had to take it. I either talk to her about it or ignore it.

T: So the "Damn it!" was different.

P: Yes. It's new to me to let it out. I still don't know how to handle it.

T: Let's look at your relationship with her in more detail.

P: To me, I do what I do best—I take care of her. I anticipate her needs and try to make things smooth and easy for her. That's how I show affection.

T: How are things with your sex life together?

P: Adequate. She doesn't like it. There's an inhibition in her, but she goes along with me.

T: What's that like for you?

P: Sometimes all right. At times I say, "The hell with it. It's more trouble than I wanted." She's aware of it and does on occasion try to smooth things over.

T: Is it a source of tension?

P: I think it is. Sometimes I want sex and she says no. I was going to say I don't think I'm unreasonable, asking too much. We used to talk about it. From our cultural background, sex is dirty. She still has that idea, so I understand.

T: How was it growing up? What did you see or hear?

P: It was always taboo. No one talked about it. It was the culture.

T: How did young people learn about it?

P: Through rumors. When a girl gets married, her mother talks to her. That would be it. In our culture, it's something you do in private. You don't talk about it. My wife's exposure was minimal.

T: What about your own?

P: In college, I went to see X-movies with friends.

T: What was that like for you?

P: It was exciting, titillating. I like to watch it when I get mad.

T: When you get mad?

P: Yes. Sex is a way of getting back at the woman.

T: You use it against your wife?

P: Not consciously, but I wouldn't be surprised if I did. It's a way to get even. It might not be out of reason to say possibly I do it to get back at my mother. It's a symbolic form of aggression.

T: What are you getting back at her for?

P: Maybe the oppression I got from her. I talked to my uncle and she let me down. Maybe that's stretching it.

T: Do you think your wish to be special had sexual overtones?

P: It never occurred to me. My thinking could be influenced by reading today why a madman behaves as he does. There might be that connection, but as far as I know, not.

(This should have been taken further.)

T: So by oppression you mean your mother dominated you, and this is a way to dominate the woman?

P: I suppose so. Maybe this is something my wife doesn't like.

T: What is that?

P: My attitude. I don't think so, but it didn't help. In the beginning, she didn't like sex at all and provoked anger in me and triggered my reaction to want to get back at my mother. It made things worse. I have tried to make it easier and pleasant for her, but it doesn't help.

T: You were frustrated by both your mother and your wife.

P: To some extent. It's something that would reinforce bottling up my emotion. I know my wife tries. It's hard to know what I can say or do. (*Silence.*) (*Sigh.*) I do feel my sex life is okay. It's not the best, but it could be worse. Maybe I'm trying to explain it away, but I think I can handle it. My feeling inhibited goes much deeper and goes back to my mother. The way my wife is doesn't help. I appreciate that she really cares for me and the kids. That's the most important thing in a marriage. At times it does irk me that she doesn't want it.

T: The other evening when you went into the bedroom and turned on the TV, were you wishing she'd be available for sex that night?

P: I don't remember. She's been under a lot of pressure at work and has been having trouble sleeping, so I tend not to raise the issue. Our normal habit is to turn on the TV, on occasions with the kids. Her attitude is let them enjoy life and don't push. Before we got married, she was very popular and I was kind of a loner. Now I have more professional friends. This week Sam and Betty and I were on a business trip and had to stay overnight. I was conscious of trying to control what I did. The principles I held to were to be myself and I made my opinions known, like where I wanted to eat. Then I'd say what they wanted was okay. Still I had some feeling of triumph that I was doing my thing.

T: How was it to be in the triangle with Betty closer to Sam?

P: I accepted the fact. It doesn't bother me. A lot of times, I went out of my way to ask for her opinion. I was aware that Sam asked her if it was too windy when she sat in the back, but he didn't ask me. They went dancing that night. I did my own thing and called my wife. I felt on my own and in control of my own destiny. I felt well-prepared for the situation.

T: You were working through what we've been talking about.

P: Yes. I think about it and what triggers what. If an event happened out of the blue, I might go back to my old way. It'll take time to change. I do feel I've begun to exert more, to take things under control at work. For one special task I've begun to bug management more for things I want, rather than passively just taking what I can get. I'm going into untested territory. I wonder how it would feel if I got bad feedback.

T: Will someone be like mother and give a negative reaction rather than a positive one?

P: Yes. I have to go through it and build up experience. I'm trying to think about my overall relationship with my family, my colleagues, everybody. When things go okay, it's hard to isolate the problem areas.

T: Do you feel any different here with me?

P: I feel more comfortable with you. *(Laughs.)* I don't know what to say. "Comfortable" is a vague word. Do you see any difference?

T: *(Smiling.)* You ask fewer questions.

(This should have been a more direct interpretation of his once again deferring to the authority of the therapist.)

P: I'm not trying to pass the buck. I feel more sure of myself. The fact that I suggest this different scenario or hypothesis and get positive feedback is encouraging. When you made the comment about my not asking questions, I felt some fear. It's still there, but it's out in the open. I can hardly wait for the time when it's not there.

T: You're still not sure if I'll be like your uncle or your mother and be angry.

P: Like the time I was able to say "Damn it" with my wife. It's a start. I want to be able to say it to someone's face, to say what my feeling is.

SESSION 25

In the twenty-fifth session the patient begins to report changes that indicate a move toward termination.

P: I handle Betty better these days. I treat her as an equal. She and Sam and I had a meeting yesterday. She was defensive when I was presenting. I was monitoring my feelings in the meeting and noted that I was uptight at the beginning. After awhile, I calmed down and then was able to carry on a conversation with Sam. He'd point out something and I could make a point or argue. It used to be all one way. He'd talk to me or I'd talk to him. Now there's some feedback. I was even able to smile a couple of times. Maybe Sam's used to my old behavior or it's his problem, but he seems uptight with me. Before, he treated others more casually and me like he's the boss and is telling me what to do. That's how I treated myself.

T: And now you are different with him.

P: I calmed myself down. I wasn't defensive. I wasn't submissive.

T: You were willing to challenge his authority.

P: *(Later in session.)* Lately, I treat Betty more as an equal, and I'm not as concerned with pleasing or placating her. It all ties in together. In the last week or two, I've tended to be more critical of people. I'm more outspoken if someone is not doing what I feel is necessary for getting the job done. . . . I would like to comment that when I feel good, I feel a lot of people respect me more.

T: Mhm.

P: That should be obvious.

T: There's a tradeoff: being specially liked or loved is exchanged for being respected as an adult.

P: I talked with my father on the phone last week. I was more blunt with him . . . not as defensive. I told him what I felt. Lately, I'm making more decisions on my own without worrying how my wife feels about it. *(She recently told him she felt he was nicer to her.)*

T: They are all tied together.

P: I'm reliving through them but with a different premise and perspective.

SESSION 26

In this session, we see the emergence of two resistances to ending treatment with the introduction of the loss issue, which came up two weeks earlier around fears that something might happen to his wife when she went on a trip alone, and the resurgence of the wish to preserve the authority figure qua authority. The positive transference necessary to the working alliance has always been manifest. We now see it as a resistance that must be dealt with quickly. Note the relevance of the opening remarks (the adaptive context).

P: I was thinking about why I was afraid to have my wife go to Washington without me. I think it's because I'm afraid of losing someone I love. As a kid, I loved my parents and they let me down. I lost them.

T: Because you were angry about that?

P: Because I stood up. They turned against me. The experience of losing someone I loved was traumatic. That's why I'm so apprehensive now.

T: The wish for your parents is still there.

P: Oh yes. It's something I want to get rid of. I want them to love me, but I don't want it to be such a burden on me.

T: You turned the angry feelings of being betrayed on yourself to keep them good, to justify them.

P: That's why, in any situation, if it doesn't go as I want, I tend to blame myself.

T: You've had to be a good boy, good student, good employee, and good patient to be specially liked as you wanted to be.

P: Yes, so I waste a lot of energy trying to be the "good boy," whatever it is. . . . I haven't yet had a chance to be relieved of the constraint to see if it would be any different.

T: Last time you were saying how it is different with Sam and Betty.

P: That's true. *(Laughs.)* Maybe I'm afraid it I take the credit for it, I will offend someone. You're right.

T: If there is a change in you, it becomes a competition of who gets the credit, you or I.

P: I consciously don't care how I get there.

T: If I get the credit, you'll still be dependent on me to recharge your batteries, as you were with Dr. L.

P: That is true.

T: Are you concerned about how I will respond if you take the credit?

P: That didn't occur to me.

T: Not consciously. How does it sound right now?

P: If I start taking the credit, I don't see how I take credit—if I notice improvement and said *I* did it?

T: Mhm.

P: It just occurred to me—I feel you'd be offended. Rather than look at the problem about who takes credit, I shift to how you feel if I do such and such. You might be offended if I take the credit. I don't look at the question, but am more concerned how people look at me.

T: How *I* look at you.

P: Right. This habit of being more afraid of offending people rather than getting into the problem and what to do about it.

T: If I am offended, I might not like you.

(T. should have added: and you might lose me as you lost your parents for standing up to them.)

P: I might know inside that I take the credit.

T: You would have that secret, but you'd still be stuck interpersonally.

P: I felt I could manipulate Dr. L. I hid the secret in me.

T: You felt good inside, but you still felt stuck with him.

P: Yes, but that isn't the case here. I'm more open and on the level with you. So far as who takes the credit, we both have credit. I'm doing the inspection and you provide the clues where and how to look. But I feel it's something I have to do myself, not something you prescribe and I swallow it.

T: Mhm.

P: That's one of my anxieties—I still hope you have that pill.

T: If you could retreat to a more passive way, you'd be less anxious.

P: Yes. It's hard to get rid of the constraints. It's partially due to my training. In technical training, you work out a solution, and if it works, it's fine. Here, there is an undoing of things that have been built up for over forty years. I mix up my wishes with my anxieties. I wonder if what I just said was trying to placate.

T: Why would you do that now?

P: Maybe deep down I still think that if I take the credit you will be offended.

T: At the beginning of our session today, you were talking about losing people who are important to you. Do you think that that concern about losing me would have to do with why you placate now? After all, if you do well and can take the credit, our work will come to an end.

(T. should have added, "And that might feel like the same kind of loss you experienced with your parents.")

P: That's entirely possible. You're the only one I can talk to and on an equal level without worrying about the consequences. So I like our relationship. On the other hand, I have a strong desire to be on my own two feet and get rid of the burdens that might hold me back. Right now, I'm talking on an intellectual level, though there is a little scared feeling. This is the kind of conversation I would like to be able to have with my wife. I do feel this kind of situation is free of constraints and I'd like to work on it at work. The question is how to do it. *(Laughs.)* Now I'm getting back into the prescription business.

Bringing the positive transference, which was becoming a resistance, into awareness enabled the patient to relocate the wish appropriately in the relationship with his wife. With a resolution of the fear of offending the therapist, the patient was able to take his full share of the credit for the improvements that resulted from treatment and, thus, become his own source of "power." This time there would be no need to return to the therapist to have his "batteries recharged."

In keeping with the thesis of this book that it is important to locate where the individual has been derailed from the developmental continuum and to determine the core relationship problem, Loewald's (1979) paper "The Waning of the Oedipus Complex" seems most relevant. He noted that while incest is the "crime" of the Oedipus complex proper, parricide is the "crime" of its dissolution. He refers to the developmental task of adolescence, the overthrow of parental authority and the assumption of responsibility for one's own life and the severing of the dependent ties of childhood. He adds that this is the essence of the superego as an internal agency. He writes: "Not only parental authority is destroyed by wresting authority from the parents and taking it over, but the parents, if the process were thoroughly carried out, are being destroyed as libidinal objects as well" (757).

In the above case presentation, it is possible to see how a less-than-perfect individuation phase with a resulting failure to solidify a sense of intrinsic power—especially the "I will"—stood in the way of achieving this developmental task of adolescence. He remained "subservient" to the will of the other. Yet, because the earlier development had been solid enough, character resistances were not a concern. The core relationship problem was played out in the transference, where it was consistently interpreted and ultimately resolved. In addition, the libidinal cathexis of his mother was appropriately brought to his relationship with his wife.

Epilogue

In 2003, I wrote the following letter to the *University of Chicago Magazine*:

As I read *The Complexity Complex* [in a previous issue of the magazine], my thoughts went to the concept's relevance to the workings of the mind. Attempts to reduce or simplify processes to neurological or biochemical factors are, in my opinion, a manifestation of a flight from the complexities that confound clinicians and nonclinicians. At the level of pop psychology, we read that men are from Mars and women are from Venus, as though this simplification would explain (and thus make controllable) the complexities of interpersonal relationships.

In the same issue *(Investigations)*, professor Michael Silverstein is reported to believe that people may be "grasping for a biological anchor for the existence of culturally and linguistically different groups" as an easy solution to the inequities in the world. What aspect of the human mind could be more uniquely complex than language through which it expresses itself?

Too often I find that the clinicians I teach and supervise seek, and almost demand, simple explanations of what makes their clients or patients so difficult to understand, work with, and help. Psychologists jump to the medical model and so join the regiment of drug-prescribing mental-health professionals. Despite the rich (and complex) literature I put before them, they want easy answers and resist the mentally taxing work of the scholarship their profession demands. (vol. 95, issue 3)

The growing focus and reliance on the medical model in the treatment of psychological problems has made it easier and easier for psychotherapists to take the easy way out. Pressure from managed-care insurance carriers and a tidal wave of advertising on radio and television by the pharmaceutical companies relieve psychotherapists across the various helping professions—including some psychoanalysts—of the discouragement of unsuccessful treatments. In my years of conducting consultation groups, I found, in particular, a countertransference resistance, a blindness to the subject of this book.

Here I have sought to delve into some of the complexities of the mind with the hope that psychotherapists who still believe in a psychology of the mind will have the help they need to persevere and help the men and women who come to them. The gratitude of the patient and the validation of their efforts should make the difficulties of the always-fascinating journey worthwhile.

References

REFERENCES

Bjerre, A. 1927. *The Psychology of Murder.* New York: DaCapo Press, 1981.

Bowlby, J. 1946. *Forty-four Juvenile Thieves: Their Character and Home-life.* London: Baillere, Tindall and Cox.

———. 1960. "Grief and Mourning in Infancy and Early Childhood." *The Psychoanalytic Study of the Child* 15: 9–52.

———. 1969. *Attachment and Loss.* Vol. 1. *Attachment.* New York: Basic Books.

———. 1973. *Attachment and Loss.* Vol. 2. *Separation: Anxiety and Anger.* New York: Basic Books.

Brenman, M. 1952. "On Teasing and Being Teased: And the Problem of 'Moral Masochism.'" In *The Psychoanalytic Study of the Child* 7: 264–85.

Evans, Berger. 1968. Antisthenes, "Diogenes Laertius VI.i." *Dictionary of Quotations.* New York: Delacorte Press, 200.

Evans, Berger. 1968. Bacon, Sir Francis. "Of Envy." *Dictionary of Quotations.* New York: Delacorte Press, 200.

Evans, Berger. 1968. Pope, Alexander. "An Essay on Man II." *Dictionary of Quotations.* New York: Delacorte Press, 201.

Bromberg, P. 1980. "Empathy, Anxiety, and Reality." *Contemporary Psychoanalysis* 16: 223–36.

———. 1983. "The Mirror and the Mask: On Narcissism and Psychoanalytic Growth." *Contemporary Psychoanalysis* 19: 359–87.

———. 1996. "Hysteria, Dissociation, and Cure: Treating Patients with Symptoms and Symptoms with Patience." *Psychoanalytic Dialogues:* 51–71.

Burgner, M., and Edgcumbe, R. 1972. "Some Problems in the Conceptualization of Early Object Relationships. Part II: The Concept of Object Constancy." *The Psychoanalytic Study of the Child* 27: 315–33.

Calogeras, R., and Alston, T. 1985. "Family Pathology and the Infantile Neurosis." *International Journal of Psychoanalysis* 66: 359–73.

Chess, S., and Thomas, A. 1971. *Temperament and Development.* New York: Brunner/Mazel.

Daniels, A. (Dr. Theodore Dalrymple.) 2001. "Anthrax Is Spread by Resentment." *The Wall Street Journal.* October 15.

Dershowitz, Alan. 1999. *Just Revenge.* New York: Warner Books.

Erikson, E. 1950. *Childhood and Society.* New York: Norton.

Etchegoyen, R., Lopez, B., and Rabin, M. 1987. "On Envy and How to Interpret It." *International Journal of Psychoanalysis* 68: 49–61.

Fantz, R. L. 1966. "Pattern Discrimination and Selective Attention as Determinants of Perceptual Development from Birth." In A. J. Kidd and J. L. Rivoire, eds. *Perceptual Development in Children.* New York: International Universities Press.

First Wives Club. 1996. Paramount Studios.

Framo, James. 1970. "Symptoms from a Family Transactional Viewpoint." *International Psychiatry Clinics*, 125–71.

Freud, A. 1965. "The Concept of Developmental Lines." *The Psychoanalytic Study of the Child* 18: 245–64.

———. 1968. "Remarks in Panel Discussion." *International Journal of Psychoanalysis* 49: 506–07.

Freud, S. [1910] 1957. "The Future Prospects of Psycho-Analytic Therapy." In J. Strachey, ed. *The Standard Edition* 11. London: Hogarth.

———. 1912. "The Dynamics of Transference." In J. Strachey, ed. *The Standard Edition* 12: 99–108. London: Hogarth.

———. [1913] 1953. "Totem and Taboo." In J. Strachey, ed. *The Standard Edition* 13. London: Hogarth.

———. [1916] 1957. "Some Character-Types Met with in Psycho-Analytic Work: Those Wrecked by Success." In J. Strachey, ed. The Standard Edition 14. London: Hogarth.

———. [1917] 1957. "General Theory of the Neuroses: Transference." In J. Strachey, ed. *The Standard Edition* 16: 431–47. London: Hogarth.

———. [1923] 1961. "The Ego and the Id." In J. Strachey, ed. *The Standard Edition* 19. London: Hogarth.

———. 1926. "Inhibitions, Symptoms, and Anxiety." In J. Strachey, ed. *The Standard Edition* 20: 77–175. London: Hogarth.

———. [1937] 1964 "Analysis Terminable and Interminable." In J. Strachey, ed. *The Standard Edition* 23. London: Hogarth.

Friedman, L. 1997. "Ferrum, Ignis, and Medicine: Return to the Crucible." *Journal of the American Psychoanalytic Association* 45: 21–36.

Giovacchini, P. 1972. *Tactics and Techniques in Psychoanalytic Therapy.* New York: Jason Aronson.

Greenberg, J. R. 1986. "Theoretical Models and the Analyst's Neutrality." *Contemporary Psychoanalysis* 22: 87–106.

Greenson, R. 1967. *The Technique and Practice of Psychoanalysis.* New York: International Universities Press.

———. 1968. "Disidentifying from Mother: Its Special Significance for Boys." In R. Greenson, *Explorations in Psychoanalysis.* New York: International Universities Press, 1978.

———. 1970. "The Unique Patient–Therapist Relationship in Borderline Patients." Presented on a panel, "The Borderline Patient," at a joint meeting of the American Psychoanalytic Association and the American Psychiatric Association. San Francisco, May.

———. 1971. "The 'Real' Relationship between the Patient and the Psychoanalyst." In R. Greenson, *Explorations in Psychoanalysis*. New York: International Universities Press, 1978, 425–40.

Grotstein, J. 1981. *Splitting and Projective Identification*. New York: Jason Aronson.

———. 1990. "Nothingness, Meaninglessness, Chaos, and the 'Black Hole' I." *Contemporary Psychoanalysis* 26: 257–90.

Haley, Jay. 1969. *The Power Tactic of Jesus Christ*. New York: Grossman.

Held-Weiss, R. 1986. "A Note on Spontaneity in the Analyst." *Contemporary Psychoanalysis* 22: 2–3.

Horner, A. [1979] 1984. *Object Relations and the Developing Ego in Therapy*. Rev. ed. Northvale, N.J.: Jason Aronson.

———. [1986, 1990] 1999. *Being and Loving*. Rev. ed. Northvale, N.J.: Jason Aronson.

———, ed. [1985] 1994. *Treating the Neurotic Patient in Brief Psychotherapy*. Northvale, N.J.: Jason Aronson.

———. 1989. *The Wish for Power and the Fear of Having It*. Northvale, N.J.: Jason Aronson.

———. 1988. "The Constructed Self and Developmental Discontinuity." *Journal of the American Academy of Psychoanalysis* 16: 235–38.

———. 1995. "The Place of the Signifier in Psychoanalytic Object Relations Therapy." *Journal of the American Academy of Psychoanalysis* 23: 71–78.

———. 1997. "Belief Systems and the Analytic Work." *American Journal of Psychoanalysis* 57: 75–78.

———. 1998. *Working with the Core Relationship Problem in Psychotherapy: A Handbook for Clinicians*. San Francisco: Jossey-Bass.

Horney, K. 1945. *Our Inner Conflicts*. New York: Norton.

———. 1950. *Neurosis and Human Growth*. New York: Norton.

Khan, M. M. R. 1963. "The Concept of Cumulative Trauma." *The Psychoanalytic Study of the Child* 18: 286–306.

Klein, M. [1957] 1975. "Envy and Gratitude." In M. Klein, *Envy and Gratitude and Other Works*. New York: Delacorte.

Kohut, H. 1971. *The Analysis of the Self*. New York: International Universities Press.

———. 1977. *The Restoration of the Self*. New York: International Universities Press.

Krystal, H. 1978. "Trauma and Affect." *The Psychoanalytic Study of the Child* 33: 81–116.

Lewis, C. S. 2001. *The Screwtape Letters*. San Francisco: Harper.

Lidz, T. and Lidz, R. 1986. "Turning Women Things into Men: Masculinization in Papua New Guinea." *Psychoanalytic Review* 73: 521–39.

Loeb, L. and Shane, M. 1982. "The Resolution of a Transsexual Wish in a Five-Year-Old Boy." *Journal of the American Psychoanalytic Association* 30: 419–34.

Loewald, H. 1979. "The Waning of the Oedipus Complex." *Journal of the American Psychoanalytic Association* 27: 751–75.

Luborsky, L., Crits-Christoph, P., Mintz, J., and Auerbach, A. 1988. *Who Will Benefit from Psychotherapy? Predicting Therapeutic Outcomes*. New York: Basic Books.

Mahler, M. 1968. *On Human Symbiosis and the Vicissitudes of Individuation.* New York: International Universities Press.

Mahler, M., Pine, F., and Bergman, A. 1975. *The Psychological Birth of the Human Infant.* New York: Basic Books.

Malan, D. H. 1976. *The Frontier of Brief Psychotherapy.* New York: Plenum Press.

Mann, J. 1973. *Time-Limited Psychotherapy.* Cambridge: Harvard University Press.

May, Rollo. 1972. *Power and Innocence.* New York: Norton.

Mayes, Linda C., and Cohen, Donald J. 1996. "Children's Developing Theory of Mind." *Journal of the American Psychoanalytic Association* 44: 117–43.

McDougall, J. 1974. "The Psychosoma and the Psychoanalytic Process." *International Review of Psycho-Analysis* 1: 437–59.

Miller, Arthur. In May (Rollo). *Power and Innocence.* New York: Norton, 47.

Milloy, S. J. 2001. *Junk Science Judo: Self-Defense Against Health Scares and Scams.* Washington, D.C.: Cato Institute.

Munn, N., Fernald, L., and Fernald, P. 1972. *Introduction to Psychology.* 3d ed. Boston: Houghton Mifflin.

Myerson, P. 1981. "When Does Need Become Desire and Desire Need?" *Contemporary Psychoanalysis* 17: 607–25.

Pally, R. 1997. "How the Brain Actively Constructs Perceptions." *International Journal of Psycho-Analysis* 78: 1021–30.

Person, E. 1997. "Review of H. K. Wrye and J. K. Welles, 'The Narration of Desire: Erotic Transferences and Countertransferences.'" *Journal of the American Psychoanalytic Association* 45: 265–70.

Poland, W. 1984. "On the Analyst's Neutrality." *Journal of the American Psychoanalytic Association* 32: 284–99.

Piaget, J. 1952. *The Origins of Intelligence in Children.* New York: International Universities Press.

Racker, H. 1957. "Contribution to the Problem of Psychopathological Stratification." *International Journal of Psycho-Analysis* 38: 223–39.

Richardson, W. 1987. "Language and Psychoanalysis." Presented in May. The American Academy of Psychoanalysis. Chicago, Illinois.

Rickles, W. 1986. "Self Psychology and Somatization: An Integration with Alexithymia." In A. Goldberg, ed. *Progress in Self Psychology.* Vol. 2. New York: Guilford.

Rowling, J. K. 1998. *Harry Potter and the Sorcerer's Stone.* New York: Scholastic, Inc.

Rutter, M. 1973. "Maternal Deprivation Reconsidered." In S. Chess and A. Thomas, eds. *Annual Progress in Child Development.* 205–16. New York: Brunner/Mazel.

———. 1974. *The Qualities of Mothering: Maternal Deprivation Reassessed.* Northvale, N.J.: Jason Aronson.

Saltzman, L. 1968. *The Obsessive Personality: Origins, Dynamics, and Therapy.* New York: Science House.

Sandler, J. 1990. "On Internal Object Relations." *Journal of the American Psychoanalytic Association* 38: 859–80.

Schafer, R. 1960. "The Loving and Beloved Superego in Freud's Structural Theory." *The Psychoanalytic Study of the Child* 15: 163–99.

———. 1983. *The Analytic Attitude.* New York: Basic Books.

Schore, A. 1996. "The Experience-Dependent Maturation of a Regulatory System in the Orbital Prefrontal Cortex and the Origin of Developmental Psychopathology." *Development and Psychopathology* 8: 59–87.

Siegel, D. 1999. *The Developing Mind: Toward a Neurobiology of Interpersonal Experience.* New York: The Guilford Press.

Sowell, T. 1998. *Late-Talking Children.* New York: Basic Books.

Sours, J. 1980. *Starving to Death in a Sea of Objects.* New York: Jason Aronson.

Stierlin, H. 1974. *Separating Parents and Adolescents: A Perspective on Running Away, Schizophrenia, and Waywardness.* New York: Quadrangle.

Stoller, R. 1975. *Perversion: The Erotic Form of Hatred.* New York: Pantheon Books.

Sullivan, H. S. 1954. *The Psychiatric Interview.* New York: Norton.

Tolpin, M. 1971. "On the Beginnings of a Cohesive Self: An Application of the Concept of Transmuting Internalization to the Study of the Transitional Object and Signal Anxiety." *The Psychoanalytic Study of the Child* 26: 316–52.

Whatever Happened to Baby Jane? 1962. Warner Brothers.

Wilson, Angus. 1974. "Introduction to *The Mystery of Edwin Drood.*" London: Penguin Books.

Winnicott, D. W. 1951. *Through Paediatrics to Psychoanalysis.* 229–42. New York: Basic Books, 1975.

———. 1965. *The Maturational Processes and the Facilitating Environment.* New York: International Universities Press.

———. 1971. *Playing and Reality.* London: Tavistock.

———. 1974. "Fear of Breakdown." *International Review of Psycho-Analysis* 1: 103–107.

Index

achievement, of identity and object constancy, 10–12, 168–69
acting out, xvi, 4, 20; of assigned role, 13; childhood and competence, relating to, 67–68; as a resistance, 49–52; sexual, xviii, 46–47; of therapist, 31, 32; transference resistance, 37; against treatment, xix, 37, 64
admiration, envy v., 74–75
adolescence: Oedipal complex, relating to, 71; opposite sex, relating to, 70–71; parents, relating to, 71; power, relating to, 70–72; therapist, relating to, 70–72
adolescent: depression in, 125; developmental tasks of, 5; therapist, relating to power of, 70–72
"affectionless psychopath," 7
aggression: power v., 54; transference resistance, relating to, 42
alexithymia, 117
anaclitical depression, ix, xix, 6, 21, 38, 60
The Analysis of the Self (Kohut), 9
analytic therapy, 43

anger, 41
anorexia nervosa: caricature of will, relating to, 120–21; core relationship problem and, 120–23; power associated with, 120–23; resistance, relating to, 120–23
anxiety: rapprochement and, 9, 10; triads of interpretation, relating to, 132
apology: confrontation, relating to, 109–11; from parents, 109–11; victim, relating to, 110–11
approach-avoidance conflict: alexithymia, relating to, 117; double approach-avoidance conflict v., 116; Oedipal stage, relating to, 118; rapprochement, relating to, 117–18; resistance, relating to, 116–18; stage of differentiation in, 116–17
attachment, process of: in developmental continuum, 5–7, 15, 60–63; as development stage, 6–7; failure of, vii, 7; sexuality and, 47; transference resistance, relating to, 7; trust/distrust, relating to, 6, 62
attributed power, 57–58
authority figures, 32–33

depression, relating to, 124; ego, relating to, 121; interminable treatment, relating to, 79; negative therapeutic reaction, relating to, 68–69; Oedipal complex, relating to, 12, 75; transference, relating to, ix, xvi, 131
friendship, 111–12
frustration, generated by envy, 73–74, 75
functions: defensive, of constructed self, 82–84; of ego, viii, 8, 23–26, 61, 63; of superego, 23, 25–26, 45
The Future Prospects of Psycho-Analytic Therapy (S. Freud), 27

gender: identification of, 49–52; transference resistance, 42–43
genital sexuality, 46–47
"good," having to be, 30
"going-on-being," 1, 60–61, 76, 116
"good boy," 35–37, 42–43, 57, 108
"good girl," 35–37, 42–43, 57
good self, 7–8, 41
government, entitlement and, 95
grandiose self, ix, 8, 9, 38–39, 40, 58, 62–63, 112
gratification, 40
Greenson, R., xvi, 31, 122
Grotstein, J., 17, 21
guilt, of constructed self, 81–86

Haley, Jay, 54
Harry Potter and the Sorcerer's Stone (Rowling), 35
hate, love v., 35
Held-Weiss, R., 31
"holding environment," 61
Horney, Karen, xviii, 22; entitlement, relating to, 94–95; projective identification, relating to, 47–48; vindictive triumph, relating to, 105–8
"How the Brain Actively Constructs Perceptions" (Pally), xxiii
hypochondriacal fears, xiv
hypothesis. *See* developmental hypothesis

"I am," 63, 70, 96
id, 39, 45, 97
identification: of gender, 49–52; projective, xvi, 47, 48
"identified patient," 13
identity: achievement of, 10–12, 168–69; language development, relating to, 10
immediacy, 129
individuation. *See* separation and individuation
interminable treatment, 79–80; Freud, relating to, 79
interpersonal relationships, 1, 9; belief systems, relating to, xxii–xxiii; object relations, relating to, xiv–xv
interpersonal triangle, 12–14, 106
interpretation: monitoring and, 130–32; of triads, 132
interpreting upward, 129–30
intransigent depression, 125
intrinsic power, 54–57; childhood and competence, relating to, 66–70; conscious sense of, 63; emotion, relating to, 55; facets of, 57; formal power v., 59; need v. desire , relating to, 96–97; shame, relating to, 63–65, 82; therapist, relating to, 56–57; transference resistance, relating to, 56–57; willpower, relating to, 55. *See also* power
Invictus, 55
irrational phenomenon, 73
"irrational role assignments," xvi, 13
I-thou encounter, viii

"junk science," xiii
Just Revenge (Dershowitz), 104

Kaczynski, Ted, 17–18
Klein, Melanie, 75–76
Kohut, H.: character resistance, relating to, xix; developmental stages, relating to, vii, ix, 5, 9, 58; structure, relating to, 21–22; transference, relating to, xix, 38, 62, 88
Krystal, H., xx, 62

About the Author

Althea J. Horner is an honorary member of the Southern California Psychoanalytic Institute and Society and a scientific associate of the American Academy of Psychoanalysis and Dynamic Psychiatry. She is listed in *Who's Who in America* and has been writing articles and books for forty years. While Dr. Horner has retired from clinical practice, she continues to write in Pasadena, California.